# 1
# The Pow

*31 Ways to a Better You*

By

# Dr. Joey N. Jones

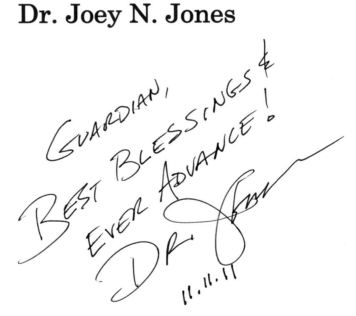

Promo Publishers
Reading that Inspires, Motivates, & Promotes Abundant Living

Silver Spring, Maryland

First Edition 2011
Copyright ©2011 Joey N. Jones, Ph.D.

All rights reserved. No part of this book may be reproduced or transmitted in any form or by any means whatsoever without express written permission from the author, except in the case of brief quotations embodied in critical articles and reviews. Please refer all pertinent questions to the publisher.

Unless otherwise indicated, all Scripture quotations are taken from the *King James Version* of the Bible.

Audrey Kinsella, Editor

Cover design by Michael Burgess

ISBN - 978-0-9831687-0-6

Promo Publishers, LLC
P.O. Box 10091
Silver Spring, Maryland 20904

Printed in the United States
Signature Book Printing, www.sbpbooks.com

# Dedication

Family is an important and inspirational part of my life. My late father (**Robert O. Jones**) and my mother (**Inez D. Jones**) taught me godly principles to live by. Their commitment to family values has shaped my character. They taught me love by loving me. So I dedicate this book to the legacy of my father and the love of my mother, who ceases not to pray for me.

Also, I dedicate this book to my brothers (**Duval, Rudy,** and **Marty**) and sisters (**Portia** and **Linda**). They continue to push forward, despite obstacles and barriers. Keep making progress!

# Acknowledgements

At the outset, I thank my beautiful wife, **Kinta,** for her insight and encouragement to complete my first of many books. She has been a constant help with her keen sense of attention to details. Also, I thank our three, lovely girls for their ideas for 100% positive words and phrases.

A lot of technical expertise is required to produce a high quality book. **Michael Burgess** provided design and art skills to create the cover that captured the essence of the book's message. I thank him for his patience and flexibility. **Audrey Kinsella** rendered excellent editing services to provide a polished finish on this project.

**Dr. Gregory Bell**, a friend and colleague is the one who planted the seed of inspiration in me 15 years ago. He gave a presentation that included a 100% word of encouragement. That seed has taken root to produce fruit in the form of this book.

I thank **Pastor A. Troy Harrison** and **First Lady Monica Harrison** for their unwavering words of support and encouragement. Their faith-filled demeanor served as a constant reminder that all things are possible to those who believe.

Mentors can be monumental. I acknowledge the mentors who have helped to shape me – **Tom Parker, Jr.**, the late **George C. Gail**, **Clifton McMullen**, **Dr. Rudy Wiggins**, and **Pastor Enoch Butler**.

Finally, I thank my Lord and Savior, **Jesus Christ**. Truly, I can do all things through Christ, which strengtheneth me.

# Disclaimer

The purpose of this book is to educate, motivate, inspire, and entertain. The author and Promo Publishers shall have neither liability nor responsibility to any person or entity with respect to any loss or damage caused, or alleged to have been caused, directly or indirectly, by the information contained in this book. This book is not endorsed by any corporation or organization noted. The views expressed in this book are those of the author.

# Table of Contents

| Chapter | | Page |
|---|---|---|
| 1 | Attitude | 9 |
| 2 | An "Aha" Advantage | 13 |
| 3 | Be a Thin King | 16 |
| 4 | Innovate | 18 |
| 5 | Five Star | 21 |
| 6 | Go an "Xtra" | 24 |
| 7 | Goals Guide | 27 |
| 8 | Leadability | 30 |
| 9 | Press In | 33 |
| 10 | Make It a #1 Brand | 35 |
| 11 | 1 Dream – I Dare You | 39 |
| 12 | 1 Change – You | 43 |
| 13 | 2 Habits 2 Break | 46 |
| 14 | 2 Habits 2 Keep | 49 |
| 15 | Plan 4 Legacy | 52 |
| 16 | Problems? | 56 |
| 17 | Develop U | 59 |
| 18 | Why Hope? | 62 |
| 19 | Get Giving | 65 |
| 20 | Speak 2 Win | 68 |
| 21 | 100% Determined | 71 |
| 22 | Higher & Above | 75 |
| 23 | No "I" in Team | 78 |

# Table of Contents (continued)

| Chapter | | Page |
|---|---|---|
| 24 | U Begin and End | 81 |
| 25 | "Ganas" & Stand | 84 |
| 26 | Academics Pay | 87 |
| 27 | Y Dn't Qt | 90 |
| 28 | Ever Advance | 93 |
| 29 | Edify Daily | 96 |
| 30 | Failure Is | 100 |
| 31 | Do It Now | 103 |

# Introduction

Motivation and inspiration can come to us in many ways. About fifteen years ago I was motivated by a gentleman giving a presentation on "attitude." Dr. Gregory Bell, a noted educator, presented the word "attitude" in such a way that I never forgot it. He expounded on the importance of having a good attitude. Then, he really captured my attention by listing each letter of the word on the board. He assigned each letter a value (A=1, B=2, C=3, etc.) according to its order in the alphabet. He concluded his presentation by adding the value of each letter. The total value was 100%. I thought, how clever! I was motivated and inspired.

Years later, Dr. Bell and I re-connected and began to dream out loud and talk about other 100% words and phrases. This spark enabled me to identify and develop over 1500 positive, 100% words and phrases. I have used these words and phrases to motivate and inspire others.

This phenomenon has been surprisingly effective in capturing the attention of the "unmotivated" and fueling their untapped drive to do better. Also, I have identified other successful people and linked their journeys to the principles behind these positive, 100% words and phrases.

I trust that you will enjoy reading this motivational and inspirational book. I believe you will find yourself seeking the next spark inside of you to do your dreams; exceed your expectations; and live life abundantly. In doing so, I believe you will touch others and multiply their drive to also undertake a positive life of service. Everybody gives something. Give your all, 100%!

The Author

## ∞ 1 ∞

# ATTITUDE = 100%

| A | B | C | D | E | F | G | H | I | J | K | L | M | N | O | P | Q | R | S | T | U | V | W | X | Y | Z |
|---|---|---|---|---|---|---|---|---|---|---|---|---|---|---|---|---|---|---|---|---|---|---|---|---|---|
| 1 | 2 | 3 | 4 | 5 | 6 | 7 | 8 | 9 | 10 | 11 | 12 | 13 | 14 | 15 | 16 | 17 | 18 | 19 | 20 | 21 | 22 | 23 | 24 | 25 | 26 |

It all begins with attitude. When you arrive to where you are going, your attitude will always precede you. Your reputation will be there, too. Attitude and reputation are first cousins. In most situations, I have gotten good results when I decided in my mind that I would put forth my best effort and face challenges with a good attitude.

Attitude is simply a way of thinking. Attitude is shaped by two things: The experiences of your senses; and which experiences you allow to take residence in your heart and mind. An attitude usually manifests itself by how you view, say, and do things. Good attitudes seek out the good; and bad attitudes attract the bad. Thus, it is vitally important what you allow through your eye gate and your ear gate. Whatever comes through these gates has the potential to park in your heart and impact your thinking and actions.

Guard your gates. Even if bad stuff gets in, don't allow it to park. Issue the bad stuff a one-way ticket out with no u-turns allowed. Welcome the good stuff and make it your friend.

You see, attitude is like planning to go to the grocery store to purchase a bag of Golden Delicious apples. When you get there, you can choose to purchase the Golden Delicious apples or you can choose to purchase lemons.

You can also choose your attitude. Regardless of the influences around you, your attitude is choice driven. I recall when I played high school basketball, I always had the attitude that we would win the game. I did not let any external circumstances change my attitude. Thus, I spoke the words of a winner. We won most of our games and tournaments. Although we did not win every single game, we were still known as winners. We talked like winners. We walked like winners. We had the attitude of a winner. We won.

David chose his attitude. It did not matter that Goliath was a champion. It did not matter that he was nearly 10-feet tall. It's not what is on the outside, but what's on the inside. Inside of David's mind, Goliath was an ant. David saw Goliath as a defeated foe.

David spoke of his victory in advance. His attitude and reputation preceded the victory over the champion. David rehearsed his previous victories. His attitude helped to frame his thinking. He reminded himself: "When I was a shepherd boy, I slew a lion and a bear, and so will be Goliath as one of them." David's attitude preceded his actions and his victory.

There are numerous principles derived from these anecdotes about the importance of attitude. One principle that stands out to me is that your actions will follow your attitude. As a leader, it is important to change attitudes if you want to genuinely change the actions of the people you lead. Words, images, and actions can help you in this quest. People respond to words because they leave a lasting imprint upon our hearts. You will read more about the importance of words in chapter 20 of this book, titled "Speak 2 Win."

Images have the potential to appeal to all five of our senses. Let's go back to the Golden Delicious apple. Do you see it? Take a bite. Now, I can tell that the apple is firm by the sound of your teeth munching away. That apple smells sweet. Now, I think you get the picture. Actions give credibility to your spoken words. If I'm constantly talking about what I am going to do and never do it, I become like a pizza delivery guy with no pizza – I don't deliver.

Attitude has an overwhelming impact on your actions. Change your attitude and you can change your actions.

> **"You can give 100% to whatever you are doing by simply choosing to have a good attitude. Your attitude can make all the difference."**

You can give 100% to whatever you are doing by simply choosing to have a good attitude. While I was attending a professional conference, the keynote speaker, famed neurosurgeon Dr. Benjamin Carson, had this to say about attitude: "I had the same brain when I was doing poorly as when I was doing well. The difference was my attitude." He was referring to how he initially performed in school as opposed to how he performs now as a neurosurgeon.

Your attitude can make all the difference. Your attitude can be the difference between getting the job done and leaving the job undone. A good attitude is vital if you expect to reap the benefits and power of giving your all. Choose a good attitude and give your all.

## ∞ 2 ∞
# An "Aha" Advantage = 100%

| A | B | C | D | E | F | G | H | I | J | K | L | M | N | O | P | Q | R | S | T | U | V | W | X | Y | Z |
|---|---|---|---|---|---|---|---|---|---|---|---|---|---|---|---|---|---|---|---|---|---|---|---|---|---|
|   |   |   |   |   |   |   |   |   |   | 1 | 1 | 1 | 1 | 1 | 1 | 1 | 1 | 1 | 2 | 2 | 2 | 2 | 2 | 2 | 2 |
| 1 | 2 | 3 | 4 | 5 | 6 | 7 | 8 | 9 | 0 | 1 | 2 | 3 | 4 | 5 | 6 | 7 | 8 | 9 | 0 | 1 | 2 | 3 | 4 | 5 | 6 |

Consider your thoughts. Do you ever think: How could things be other than they are? I believe there are at least one million more inventions to be made; discoveries to be uncovered; and solutions to be shared in order to improve our lives. When you think otherwise, you give yourself an "aha" advantage – this is confident thinking that results in a joyful surprise of triumph and clarity of understanding.

The word "aha" dates back to biblical times, as recorded in Isaiah 44:16. Here, aha is used to illustrate how one man builds an idol made of wood and yet, he uses the same wood to burn in order to produce heat. The text in its entirety explains the folly of idolatry. The moment of clarity in thinking leads the man to understand that the wood is beneficial to him when it is burned to warm his body.

An aha advantage begins with your thinking. Have you ever wondered about the development of the simple paper clip? Before its invention, people would cut parallel slits in the corner of a stack of papers and bind them with waxed ribbons. This method was used for over 600 years, until William D. Middlebrook invented the modern-day gem clip in 1899. Now, there are others who are given credit for various versions of this simple, yet functional device. They include Samuel Fay (who holds an 1867 patent for a ticket fastener that was also used to fasten papers together); Johan Vaaler, a Norwegian (who holds an 1899 German patent for his paper clip invention); Cornelius J. Brosnan (who was awarded a patent in 1900 for his invention of the "konaclip"); and George McGill (who holds a 1903 patent for a version of a paper clip). The question arises: Why did it take so long for these persons to think otherwise? Aha, I think I have the answer.

> **"Two of the planet's greatest assets are thinking and believing."**

Two of the planet's greatest assets are thinking and believing. The thought of one person can ignite the thinking of many. This aha advantage principle can be developed by looking at the way things are and then thinking about how they could or should be.

Oprah Winfrey, the multi-millionaire, and talk-show host, thinks that aha moments are important and life-changing. In fact, she highlights an aha moment in each issue of her *O Magazine*.

Again, think about the invention of the paper clip and its impact on our lives, every day. Eighteen billion paper clips are used annually just in the United States. That's impact. That's the result of an aha advantage. What will be your next aha moment that leads to an aha advantage? Think about it.

## ∞ 3 ∞

# Be a Thin King = 100%

| A | B | C | D | E | F | G | H | I | J | K | L | M | N | O | P | Q | R | S | T | U | V | W | X | Y | Z |
|---|---|---|---|---|---|---|---|---|---|---|---|---|---|---|---|---|---|---|---|---|---|---|---|---|---|
| 1 | 2 | 3 | 4 | 5 | 6 | 7 | 8 | 9 | 10 | 11 | 12 | 13 | 14 | 15 | 16 | 17 | 18 | 19 | 20 | 21 | 22 | 23 | 24 | 25 | 26 |

Problems and challenges are inevitable. They force us to grow or to fail. One summer afternoon, I was working on the lawn. Somehow, the lawnmower's starting mechanism broke. I did not want to replace the entire lawnmower for a part that costs less than five dollars. I went to several stores to locate the part. Initially, I was unsuccessful. However, I did find a part that was very similar to what I was looking for. But, I did not think it would work properly so I decided to continue my quest. Again, I was unsuccessful.

After about two hours of frustration I returned home and went back to the drawing board. I began to think about other ways of accomplishing my goal. I located the broken part and studied it. I learned that the purpose of the part was to transfer power to the engine via the spark plug to make the lawnmower start.

I then asked myself questions and began to think out loud. What seemed to be a difficult task, turned out to be quite simple, because I began to be a thin king. That's right – "BE A THIN KING." The principle behind this

100% phrase is that many of our solutions lie within us, but only if we will begin to think otherwise. Be a thin king. Thinking can put you on top.

> **"Your choices are unlimited when failure is not an option."**

Being a thin king also involves exercising your mind. Always keep your mind open to choices. Your choices are unlimited when failure is not an option. Ideas can begin to flow like the Nile. Don't let go of your ability to stay open. Stay available. Remain optimistic. Keep thinking. Be a thin king and receive royal rewards. This is the power of giving your all.

## ∞ 4 ∞

# Innovate = 100%

| A | B | C | D | E | F | G | H | I | J | K | L | M | N | O | P | Q | R | S | T | U | V | W | X | Y | Z |
|---|---|---|---|---|---|---|---|---|---|---|---|---|---|---|---|---|---|---|---|---|---|---|---|---|---|
| 1 | 2 | 3 | 4 | 5 | 6 | 7 | 8 | 9 | 10 | 11 | 12 | 13 | 14 | 15 | 16 | 17 | 18 | 19 | 20 | 21 | 22 | 23 | 24 | 25 | 26 |

Worldwide sales exceeded $25 billion in 2008. Their products are sold in nearly 200 countries. They provide employment for more than 79,000 people. Their singular commitment is to make life easier and better for people around the world. Who am I talking about? It is none other than the Minnesota Mining and Manufacturing Company, better known as 3M.

In 1902, five businessmen (two railroad employees, a meat market proprietor, a lawyer, and a doctor) banded together to form 3M. Their original plan was to sell mineral corundum to be used for making grinding wheels. 3M has thrived for more than 100 years and continues to grow. Today, 3M is one of the 30 companies which make up the Dow Jones Industrial Average and it is a member of the S&P 500.

A pillar of the company's foundation is innovation. I believe that their ability to innovate is a key component to their success. They develop an array of products including sandpaper, masking tape, graphic arts materials, cleaning pads, health care and dental products, overhead projector systems, duct tape, optical films for LCD televisions, and yes, Post-It notes.

How do you foster a culture in which innovation is expected and respected? I believe the answer is found in the company's values. There are three of the six 3M values that really capture my attention when you talk about innovation.

The first value is: "Act with uncompromising honesty and integrity in everything we do." This value sets the tone for clear and uninhibited thinking that places the needs of others ahead of one's own.

Secondly, another value states: "Respect our social and physical environment around the world." I believe you should not solve one problem, while creating others in the process.

> **"If you want the ability to innovate, start to develop the ability of your people."**

"Value and develop our employees' diverse talents, initiative and leadership" is the third value. Without people, there is no program, process, progress, or profit.

It is quite noticeable that all three of these values focus on the development of people. If you want the ability to innovate, start to develop the ability of your people. William L. McKnight, who served as 3M's chairman of the board from 1949 to 1966 said, "Mistakes will be made. But if a person is essentially right, the mistakes he or she makes are not as serious in the long run as the mistakes management makes if it undertakes to tell those in authority, exactly how they must do their jobs." Are you allowing yourself and others to be innovative? Why or why not?

Finally, what are you developing in you, in order to help meet the needs of others? Tap into the power of giving your all. Innovate.

## ∞ 5 ∞
# Five Star = 100%

| A | B | C | D | E | F | G | H | I | J | K | L | M | N | O | P | Q | R | S | T | U | V | W | X | Y | Z |
|---|---|---|---|---|---|---|---|---|---|---|---|---|---|---|---|---|---|---|---|---|---|---|---|---|---|
|   |   |   |   |   |   |   |   |   |   | 1 | 1 | 1 | 1 | 1 | 1 | 1 | 1 | 1 | 2 | 2 | 2 | 2 | 2 | 2 | 2 |
| 1 | 2 | 3 | 4 | 5 | 6 | 7 | 8 | 9 | 0 | 1 | 2 | 3 | 4 | 5 | 6 | 7 | 8 | 9 | 0 | 1 | 2 | 3 | 4 | 5 | 6 |

"A gold and alabaster chandelier; a dazzling hand-painted sky motif ceiling; a grand piano; beautiful hand-woven tapestries-- all perfectly accented with Empire Period furnishings. Paneled entry doors lead the way to airy rooms. Nine-foot ceilings, crown moldings and plush carpeting add to the ambience."

These are just some of the amenities indicative of a five-star hotel. The five-star rating system is commonly used to rank or categorize hotels, restaurants, movies, cars, TV shows, safety features, musical work, performances, and military status.

I have had the good fortune of staying in a five-star hotel. Beginning with my arrival and until my departure, it was absolutely luxurious and impressive. I was greeted with a genuine smile. Somehow, the bellhop knew my name. I felt like I was a dignitary. Immediately, I knew I would have a most enjoyable stay. Everything was authentic. Everything was far beyond the norm or ordinary. Simply put, it was extraordinary. I would not hesitate to go there again.

Hotels and other entities have rating systems, but what about us? How do you or others rate your life?

Do you greet people with a genuine smile? When a person meets you, would that person want to meet you again? I believe that the foundation for a five-star life is one's emanating superb human relations skills. It is the people that add value to an establishment. A five-star hotel gets its rating based on the physical substance <u>and</u> how the staff members serve the guests. Sensational service produces patrons and continuous customers.

What characteristics do you currently possess that make you a five-star person? Whatever they are, they should be valuable and helpful to someone else. Identify them and build upon them. At least one of your characteristics should be the capability and drive to provide exceptional service. Your service to people should be like a magnet attracting them to you.

> "Your service to people should be like a magnet attracting them to you. How's your service? Would someone rate you as five-star?"

How's your service? Would someone rate you as five-star?

Another characteristic of a five-star hotel is the high price. The finer things in life cost. Which leads to the question: What are you willing to give up for a season in order to get something valuable that lasts for a lifetime? A five-star hotel does not happen overnight. It is purposely planned. Are you planning a five-star life?

See yourself as a five-star person. Then, present yourself as a five-star person and do the things that are characteristic of a five-star person. For example, greet people with a genuine smile; seek to meet the needs of others; add value to your relationships. Ironically, these actions cost very little, but could yield high dividends. Give it your all.

Finally, one way of giving your all is to apply the familiar principle of doing unto others as you would have them do unto you. My stay at that five-star hotel would have been worthless without the service that I received from the five-star people who worked there. You can be a five-star person and have a five-star life. This is the power of giving your all.

## ∞ 6 ∞

# Go an "Xtra" = 100%

| A | B | C | D | E | F | G | H | I | J | K | L | M | N | O | P | Q | R | S | T | U | V | W | X | Y | Z |
|---|---|---|---|---|---|---|---|---|---|---|---|---|---|---|---|---|---|---|---|---|---|---|---|---|---|
| 1 | 2 | 3 | 4 | 5 | 6 | 7 | 8 | 9 | 10 | 11 | 12 | 13 | 14 | 15 | 16 | 17 | 18 | 19 | 20 | 21 | 22 | 23 | 24 | 25 | 26 |

You must do what is required or expected before you can go the extra mile.

Do you know anyone who goes above and beyond what is expected? This person can be considered to be an "extra mile" person. Actually, the concept of going the extra mile is first recorded in the Bible, found in the Book of Matthew, the fifth chapter, verse 41. Some say that the first mile represents what you are supposed to do. The extra mile represents your passion for what you do or for your love and care for a person or thing.

If you "go an xtra" mile, it can make all the difference. I recall a time when I was in a hospital waiting room with my wife. She was in excruciating pain and very sensitive to noise. The medical assistants and staff were very pleasant and professional. Several hospital attendants were doing their required jobs by pushing and rolling hospital apparatus throughout the hallway and in the process, contributing to the noise and unknowingly contributing to my wife's pain.

Immediately, I thought about the principle of going the extra mile. If I were a hospital administrator, what would I do to address the issue of the noise and make the environment better? Carefully analyzing the situation, I realized that the squeaky wheels and the slamming of doors accounted for most of the noise. I had a solution. A few squirts of WD-40® on the squeaky wheels and the use of common courtesy when opening and closing the doors could make all the difference.

You don't want to be known for the noise that you make, but for the difference you make. I believe this story illustrates the principle of going the extra mile. When a person goes the extra mile, he or she renders better quality service than what is required or expected.

> **"You must do what is required or expected before you can go the extra mile."**

The late Napoleon Hill, famed motivational writer and author of *Think and Grow Rich*, explained the principle of going the extra mile in a formula. He said: "The QQMA formula can afford a person to write his or her own ticket and make sure of getting it." The QQMA formula consists of three components: 1) **Q**uality of service that you render; 2) **Q**uantity of service that you render; and 3) **M**ental **A**ttitude in which you render your service.

Hill also outlined at least 15 benefits that result from going the extra mile. One of my favorites is the benefit of influencing others to respect your integrity, thus leading to their willingness to go out of their way to support or cooperate with you in a friendly spirit. Wow! This is awesome. Why not make up in your mind to do more than is required? You will be helping others and yourself. You will reap far more than you give.

Furthermore, your work will be more enjoyable and promote an atmosphere of harmony and productivity. This is the power of giving your all. Go an "xtra" mile. You really can't afford not to.

## ∞ 7 ∞
# Goals Guide = 100%

| A | B | C | D | E | F | G | H | I | J | K | L | M | N | O | P | Q | R | S | T | U | V | W | X | Y | Z |
|---|---|---|---|---|---|---|---|---|---|---|---|---|---|---|---|---|---|---|---|---|---|---|---|---|---|
|   |   |   |   |   |   |   |   |   |   | 1 | 1 | 1 | 1 | 1 | 1 | 1 | 1 | 1 | 2 | 2 | 2 | 2 | 2 | 2 | 2 |
| 1 | 2 | 3 | 4 | 5 | 6 | 7 | 8 | 9 | 0 | 1 | 2 | 3 | 4 | 5 | 6 | 7 | 8 | 9 | 0 | 1 | 2 | 3 | 4 | 5 | 6 |

Goals provide the foundation for direction, purpose, and destiny. Direction or "where" you are going is vital in meeting any goal. Purpose provides the "why" of what you are doing. Destiny is the "how" and "what" of your journey. Thus, goals may be defined as **g**uiding **o**pportunities **a**t **l**ife's **s**uccesses.

The size of your goal may also be an indication of the degree of challenge and complexity required to meet and even exceed this opportunity. Goals are good. They prompt you to grow. Goals are even more exciting when they spill over into the lives of others, causing them to experience a level of success that they never even imagined was possible.

Dr. Benjamin Carson, famed neurosurgeon, had this to say about goals, while responding to interview questions posed to him by the Academy of Achievement organization: "The most important thing to me is taking your God-given talents and developing them to the utmost, so that you can be useful to your fellow-man, period."

Dr. Carson continued to expound,

> The thing that really motivates me right now, to be honest with you, is the opportunity to get other people to understand what's important in life. What's important in their life, and what's important in the life of our society and in the life of the nation? I really believe that that's what civilization is all about. And, it doesn't have a whole lot to do, quite frankly, with the accumulation of wealth, and titles, and degrees, and power. Even though, interestingly enough, when you do develop your God-given talents and you become valuable, you know, those things just seem to accumulate. But that should not be a person's goal. The goal should be to become a valuable individual, and I believe that that's what success is all about. And the more people we can get to understand that, the better off we're going to be as a nation.

Certainly, Dr. Carson understands how his goals impact the lives of others. So, one of the strategies of giving your all is to develop goals that develop your life and positively impact the lives of others. An important step to this end is to write down your goals.

The process of writing down your goals allows you to review your goals and make adjustments and take actions, as necessary.

> **"...goals may be defined as guiding opportunities at life's successes."**

Finally, remember, goals can give you direction, purpose, and destiny. Write them down. Developing written goals sounds like a winning combination for life and achieving a better you. Goals can help you experience the power of giving your all.

Every idea needs goals in order for it to take off. Goals give your ideas wings. Without goals, you could end up nowhere. A person without a goal is like a ship tossed to and fro, ending up lost at sea and alone. Goals give you direction and purpose for your actions.

What are your goals? Are your goals guiding you? If not, start fresh. Develop goals. Write them down. This is the power of giving your all.

## ∞ 8 ∞

# Leadability = 100%

| A | B | C | D | E | F | G | H | I | J | K | L | M | N | O | P | Q | R | S | T | U | V | W | X | Y | Z |
|---|---|---|---|---|---|---|---|---|---|---|---|---|---|---|---|---|---|---|---|---|---|---|---|---|---|
| 1 | 2 | 3 | 4 | 5 | 6 | 7 | 8 | 9 | 10 | 11 | 12 | 13 | 14 | 15 | 16 | 17 | 18 | 19 | 20 | 21 | 22 | 23 | 24 | 25 | 26 |

I believe that one of the most pressing issues facing America and even the world is the lack of leadership. I'm talking about people who are called or needed to provide leadership and are hesitant to do so. For example, according to a 2004 U.S. Census Bureau report, over 25 million children lived without their biological father residing in the household. That is roughly 1 out of every 3 (34.5%) children in America.

The numbers are even more startling when we account for race. Nearly 2 in 3 (65%) African American children were living without their fathers. Nearly 4 in 10 (35%) Hispanic children lived without their fathers. And nearly 3 in 10 (27%) white children lived in a father-absent household. And, listen to this: In 2001, over 150 schools in New York City opened with only a temporary principal at the helm. Leadership, come forth!

Just as excellent leadership has a positive impact on its followers and surrounding people, poor leadership or vacant leadership has a negative effect on the people. The by-products of poor leadership include stunted growth, loss of revenue, and a culture that misses and avoids opportunities to go to the next dimension.

When an organization goes to the next dimension, it moves upward and expands outward. Thus, more room is created for more people to lead. When the right people are in charge, the people rejoice!

> "What can you do to develop your "leadability"? I define leadability as the desire to develop others such that your abilities are inevitably developed, too."

More people should be rejoicing because of the right people being in leadership. When the right people are in leadership, they perpetuate success. Thus, one of the fundamental responsibilities of leaders should be to recruit and prepare the next generation to lead.

Such is a problem of the nonprofit business sector and many other nonprofit organizations in this country. Oftentimes, there is a lack of a succession plan for leadership. What's more, there is potentially an absence of leaders, people who are willing to step up to the plate in the near future. Take, for example, a recent study which estimated that the nonprofit industry will need to hire an additional 640,000 executives through the year 2016.

In addition, developing the "right" leadership is critical. How do we do so? Every leader must look at this question: What can you do to develop your "leadability"? I define leadability as the desire to develop others such that your abilities are inevitably developed, too, not to mention shared with younger or newer leaders.

Here is an action step to realize this goal. If you are a leader within your organization, then co-author an article or newsletter with a new hire. This could be the scenario: You have the experience. The new hire has the writing skills and ability for producing good written expression about your experience. Inevitably, both parties will win and benefit from this paired effort.

This is the concept of leadability put into action. When this scenario or concept is replicated throughout an organization, the business flourishes and the leader's life's legacy continues. This is the power of giving your all.

## ∞ 9 ∞
# Press In = 100%

| A | B | C | D | E | F | G | H | I | J | K | L | M | N | O | P | Q | R | S | T | U | V | W | X | Y | Z |
|---|---|---|---|---|---|---|---|---|---|---|---|---|---|---|---|---|---|---|---|---|---|---|---|---|---|
|   |   |   |   |   |   |   |   |   |   | 1 | 1 | 1 | 1 | 1 | 1 | 1 | 1 | 1 | 2 | 2 | 2 | 2 | 2 | 2 | 2 |
| 1 | 2 | 3 | 4 | 5 | 6 | 7 | 8 | 9 | 0 | 1 | 2 | 3 | 4 | 5 | 6 | 7 | 8 | 9 | 0 | 1 | 2 | 3 | 4 | 5 | 6 |

Remember, when you feel like giving up, it's only a feeling. Choose to replace the feeling with a decision. Decide to give more; decide to give it another try; decide to give it your all. Press in. You can't allow a little pressure to put down your hopes and dreams.

However, not all pressure is bad. Pressure produces wine from grapes; diamonds from coal; and extraordinary from ordinary. What will pressure produce from you? Use pressure for your good. In other words, pressure can bring out your very best. Press in.

When pressing in, don't be discouraged by what you see. I find it quite interesting that some people can look at a potentially negative situation and get upset. Others will look at the same situation and see it as a set up, a set up for something good to happen. So, watch what you see.

Overcome negative pressure with purpose. I have observed that when I am overwhelmed with pressure, usually I am off purpose. When your life and actions are driven by purpose, pressure becomes fuel for focus. You pause and take inventory of what is most important. You eliminate the extra actions and time-busters which add up to little or no value.

> "Pressure produces wine from grapes; diamonds from coal; and extraordinary from ordinary. What will pressure produce from you?"

Consider the successful life of Glen W. Bell, Jr., founder of Taco Bell®. On the heels of economic recessions in the early 1960s, he experienced some pressure while trying to compete with hamburger giant, McDonald's, which was located a few miles from his own drive-in hamburger and hotdog stand. The pressure prompted him to do something differently. In 1962, with a $4000 investment, he opened the first Taco Bell®. In 1978, he sold the business to PepsiCo for about $125 million.

Pressure today could mean millions tomorrow. Press in. This is the power of giving your all.

## ∞ 10 ∞
## Make It a #1 Brand = 100%

| A | B | C | D | E | F | G | H | I | J | K | L | M | N | O | P | Q | R | S | T | U | V | W | X | Y | Z |
|---|---|---|---|---|---|---|---|---|---|---|---|---|---|---|---|---|---|---|---|---|---|---|---|---|---|
| 1 | 2 | 3 | 4 | 5 | 6 | 7 | 8 | 9 | 10 | 11 | 12 | 13 | 14 | 15 | 16 | 17 | 18 | 19 | 20 | 21 | 22 | 23 | 24 | 25 | 26 |

Many people share the belief that Rolex holds the crown when it comes to luxury watches. Why is this so? What sets Rolex apart from the crowd? Why do presidents, champions, and dignitaries prefer the Rolex brand?

Let's begin with the founder and visionary, Hans Wilsdorf. In 1905, Hans Wilsdorf and his brother-in-law, Alfred Davis, founded a business called "Wilsdorf and Davis." Basically, they imported watch parts, assembled them, and sold them to jewelers. Wilsdorf and Davis usually put their mark ("W&D") on the inside of the case-back. I believe that something special happens when someone places their name on a product or service. In most cases, it sends a message of unwavering quality and dedication to excellence. It gives you the extra fuel to continue to produce at a very high level. It sends a message to the customer. You would recognize the product or service even if the name were absent.

The word "Rolex" has even become synonymous with luxury and high quality. One claim regarding the word's origin, notes that Alfred Davis developed the word. Alfred Davis drove a Rolls Royce and wanted the watch to have the same message of exquisite, high quality. So, he used the letters "rol" from the automobile and added "ex" from the well-known Timex watch brand to form "Rolex." There are multiple stories depicting the origin of the word, but undeniably there is one message delivered – luxury and high quality. To put its quality to the test, Rolex advertised that their watches were waterproof, and the company proved this claim by submerging its watches in an aquarium in store-front windows.

Rolex has distanced itself from the crowd by being a leader in watchmaking innovation. Rolex developed the first waterproof watch case; the first watch with a date on the dial; the first watch to display two time zones at once; and it was the first watchmaker to earn its product certification as a chronometer. Rolex has set the standard for time. This is why people from all over the globe crown Rolex as the king of luxury watches.

Another product that comes to mind when I think about brand is Nike®. NIKE, Inc., is the world's leading supplier of athletic shoes, with revenue exceeding $18 billion in 2008. In 1964, NIKE, Inc., was founded by Philip Knight, a track athlete at the University of Oregon, and his coach Bill Bowerman.

The company's original name was Blue Ribbon Sports. The current company's name was derived from the

Greek goddess Nike, which means victory. And speaking of victory, it is virtually impossible to focus on Nike® without thinking about Michael Jordan, one of the best basketball players of all time.

Jordan, winner of six NBA championships, catapulted the Nike® brand name to fame in 1985, with the release of Air Jordan I, or known affectionately as "Jordans." Made of high-quality Italian leather, the Nike® Air Jordan brand is known throughout the world. The Air Jordan brand has style and a story. Oftentimes the designs would tell a story of Michael's life and accomplishments. Michael Jordan retired from playing basketball after the 2002-2003, season, yet the Air Jordan brand continues its standing as the number one athletic shoe brand in the world.

> "...something special happens when someone places their name on a product or service. In most cases, it sends a message of unwavering quality and dedication to excellence."

Rolex is known for high quality, luxury watches. Nike® is known for high quality, stylish athletic shoes.

What are you known for? What type of brand are you? We may not know what it is yet, but we really should think about this and set about creating one.

How do you develop your brand as a person? Normally, we know products and services by their brand, but we know people by their character and reputation. You can develop your personal brand by giving your all, giving 100% on a consistent basis. There is power in giving your all. Most people appreciate a valiant effort. Develop a habit and practice of giving your all. It may very well lead to a number one brand.

## ∞ 11 ∞
# 1 Dream − I Dare You = 100%

| A | B | C | D | E | F | G | H | I | J | K | L | M | N | O | P | Q | R | S | T | U | V | W | X | Y | Z |
|---|---|---|---|---|---|---|---|---|---|---|---|---|---|---|---|---|---|---|---|---|---|---|---|---|---|
|   |   |   |   |   |   |   |   |   |   | 1 | 1 | 1 | 1 | 1 | 1 | 1 | 1 | 1 | 2 | 2 | 2 | 2 | 2 | 2 | 2 |
| 1 | 2 | 3 | 4 | 5 | 6 | 7 | 8 | 9 | 0 | 1 | 2 | 3 | 4 | 5 | 6 | 7 | 8 | 9 | 0 | 1 | 2 | 3 | 4 | 5 | 6 |

Have you ever dreamed that you were successful or more successful than you are now?

A dream can be described as an image, emotion, idea, or vision occurring involuntarily in one's mind while asleep. Dreams can also occur while one is totally awake and envisions what might or could be. It is quite interesting that oneirologists (that is, persons who study dreams) have discovered that most involuntary dreams occur during a time of sleep known as rapid eye movement (REM) sleep. In addition to the eyes moving at a rapid pace, the brain activity is measurably increased. Our thinking is increased when we dream.

> "There are 8760 hours in a year. If you take just one hour to dream how you spend the other 8759 hours, it could make all the difference for the rest of your life."

Dream research indicates that we can influence our involuntary dreams by what we do in life and how we think. This is more evident by what we do just before going to sleep. What enters your ear gate or eye gate before you go to sleep?

Take a lesson from people who have dreamed of and achieved success. Many such people have credited their success to God-given dreams and the corresponding actions that made their dream a reality. For one good example, take famed scientist George Washington Carver, who said that "the Great Creator" revealed his ideas for planting and developing the peanut, the sweet potato, and the pecan.

For another example, take note that one of the greatest inventors of all times, Thomas Edison, revealed that he got the idea for the phonograph in a dream. Edison in fact is credited with obtaining over 1090 patents for new products.

Another example: In 1964, renowned golfer Jack Nicklaus said this to a reporter: "Wednesday night I had a dream and it was about my golf swing. I was hitting them pretty good in the dream and all at once I realized I wasn't holding the club the way I've actually been holding it lately. I've been having trouble collapsing my right arm taking the club head away from the ball, but I was doing it perfectly in my sleep. So when I came to the course yesterday morning, I tried it the way I did in my dream and it worked. I shot a sixty-eight yesterday and a sixty-five today."

And yet another example is this: In 1965, singer and songwriter, Paul McCartney woke up one morning from a dream with a classical string ensemble performing in his head; and the song, "Yesterday" was birthed. The <u>Guinness Book of Records</u> notes that this Beatles song has the most cover versions of any song ever written and, according to record label BMI, it was performed over seven million times in the 20th century.

And let's not forget that King Solomon received wisdom from God in a dream on how to lead his people. That wisdom also reaped riches and wealth untold.

These are only a few examples of how just one dream can change our lives and impact the people around us. Don't discount your dreams. Live them.

Are you birthing your dreams? Or, are your dreams still in the incubator? Some dreams have been in the incubator too long. Yes, there is the old adage "Sleep on it." But, when you wake up, it's time to act. It's time to launch your dreams.

There are 8760 hours in a year. If you take just one hour to dream how you spend the other 8759 hours, it could make all the difference for the rest of your life.

Just be careful. Every dream is not your destiny. Certainly, you must discern which dreams are inspired and which ones are inquired. Inspired dreams require faith and actions to bring to fruition. Inquired dreams are simply feel-good notions. Be inspired. Take time to dream one dream. I dare you. This is the power of giving your all.

## ∞ 12 ∞
# 1 Change - You = 100%

| A | B | C | D | E | F | G | H | I | J | K | L | M | N | O | P | Q | R | S | T | U | V | W | X | Y | Z |
|---|---|---|---|---|---|---|---|---|---|---|---|---|---|---|---|---|---|---|---|---|---|---|---|---|---|
| 1 | 2 | 3 | 4 | 5 | 6 | 7 | 8 | 9 | 10 | 11 | 12 | 13 | 14 | 15 | 16 | 17 | 18 | 19 | 20 | 21 | 22 | 23 | 24 | 25 | 26 |

Change is what you make it. We oftentimes want people to change something in order to meet our needs or wants. Ever considered one very important change – namely, you? If you are not living the life you envisioned, then change your outlook. If you are not impacting the lives of other people, the question is: Why?

In June of 2009, President Barack Obama asked the question: "How are you delivering on change?" This is a profound question. He prompted us to consider ourselves as agents of change by living a life of service and volunteerism in our local communities.

You can act on this change today. But remember: change can be defined as the process of becoming different. Also, I submit to you, what are you doing to make a difference? What are you doing today that you have never done before? Have you ever read a book to a child? Ever donated time in a nursing home? Ever given away a thousand dollars? Doing something different precedes change.

I am convinced that some people resist change because they are comfortable with the "good ole days." However, there's one problem. The good ole days are in the past. We live in the now and later. Dr. Michael Freeman, a well-known and respected pastor, put it this way: "When your memories outweigh your vision, you are just about done."

> "...when you make progress and achieve your goals, be satisfied for a moment. Then, go back to work because change is looking to arrest your best, today, and make it mediocre, tomorrow."

If you want to maintain the status quo, things will have to change. If you want to change the status quo, things will have to change. Whether you do something or nothing, things will change. We can't escape the laws of change.

Consider doing something that transforms, replaces, alters, modifies, substitutes, switches, or reverses the outcome. And remember, when you make progress and achieve your goals, be satisfied for a moment. Then, go back to work because change is looking to arrest your best, today, and make it mediocre, tomorrow. Consider making one change – you. You can do it. This is the power of giving your all.

## ∞ 13 ∞
# 2 Habits 2 Break = 100%

| A | B | C | D | E | F | G | H | I | J | K | L | M | N | O | P | Q | R | S | T | U | V | W | X | Y | Z |
|---|---|---|---|---|---|---|---|---|---|---|---|---|---|---|---|---|---|---|---|---|---|---|---|---|---|
| 1 | 2 | 3 | 4 | 5 | 6 | 7 | 8 | 9 | 10 | 11 | 12 | 13 | 14 | 15 | 16 | 17 | 18 | 19 | 20 | 21 | 22 | 23 | 24 | 25 | 26 |

What's a factor in how we use our time? Where we spend our money? How we approach challenges? Why we succeed or fail? Are all of these done according to well-worn habits that we have? What about these habits?

Our habits play a major role in our lives. Developing good habits can be critical to our success. Let me explain. An employee who has a good habit of arriving to work on time and doing more than is required may be in line for a big promotion. Quite frankly, it pays to have good habits.

Simply put, a habit may be described as a repeated behavior. Oftentimes, habits are done subconsciously or without our even thinking about them. Habits are like diamonds. They are hard to break, but they can be profitable if developed for good purposes. So, habits just don't happen. They are developed by exposure to stimuli, over time.

"Challenging" is the word that describes the task of trying to determine two habits to break. There are many bad habits surrounding our lives. But, look up! There is good news. You can break a bad habit. Here are two habits that need to be broken: speaking defeat and failing to try.

Speaking defeat is actually an emotion so strong and abundant in one's heart that one will focus on the one-percent chance of failure rather than think about the ninety-nine-percent certainty of success. Thus, if opportunity met that person today and offered a chance at success, the person will often say, "No, I can't do it." If you have a habit of speaking defeat, you can change your confession. Change the way you speak. The same number of muscles it takes to say "no" is the same number of muscles it takes to say "yes." Try it.

Maxwell Maltz, plastic surgeon and self-help guru, says, "To change a habit, make a conscious decision, then act out the new behavior." Yes, it sounds simple, but you have got to start somewhere. Try it!

Failing to try is another habit to break. You may not ever know what you can become until you try to become it. Trying moves you that much closer to becoming. The late, William Arthur Ward, a well-known writer of inspirational quotes, once said, "The greatest failure is the failure to try." I submit to you that when you "**try**" something, you actually **t**ake a **r**isk on **y**ou. Certainly, you are worth trying! Choosing to always play it "**safe**" is simply **s**taying **a**t **f**ailure to **e**xcel.

Begin your victory over the terrible habit of failing to try by saying to yourself, "I will give it a try." You must decide what the "it" will be. It could be your words! What will be your next words that lead to victory in your life? What will be your next attempt at trying something new that leads to success in your life? Say it and do it! Find the hidden treasure buried in your heart. You can do it. This is the power of giving your all.

## ∞ 14 ∞
## 2 Habits 2 Keep = 100%

| A | B | C | D | E | F | G | H | I | J | K | L | M | N | O | P | Q | R | S | T | U | V | W | X | Y | Z |
|---|---|---|---|---|---|---|---|---|---|---|---|---|---|---|---|---|---|---|---|---|---|---|---|---|---|
|   |   |   |   |   |   |   |   |   |   | 1 | 1 | 1 | 1 | 1 | 1 | 1 | 1 | 1 | 1 | 2 | 2 | 2 | 2 | 2 | 2 |
| 1 | 2 | 3 | 4 | 5 | 6 | 7 | 8 | 9 | 0 | 1 | 2 | 3 | 4 | 5 | 6 | 7 | 8 | 9 | 0 | 1 | 2 | 3 | 4 | 5 | 6 |

Research by Dr. Maxwell Maltz, a cosmetic surgeon and developer of Psycho-Cybernetics, which is a system of ideas that he claimed could improve one's self-image, discovered that 21 days is the magic number to develop or break a habit, good or bad. He noticed that a change in one's mind-set led to a change in self-image that rendered plastic surgery unnecessary for some of his patients who believed plastic surgery was the answer for their problems. He believed that when the brain was bombarded with the same behavior or stimuli for 21 straight days, a habit was formed. He noticed this phenomenon during his work with amputees.

Why not take the next three weeks to develop your next good habit? For example, if you are in sales, you could make it a habit to find out what you and your next client have in common. A personal touch could mean more profits.

Now, what are some good habits to keep? Live wealthy. This is one of at least two habits to keep. Living wealthy means living a life that is so valuable that everything you do benefits you <u>and</u> others. Wealth is not measured in money alone.

However, money *is* an answer to many things. Live wealthy is a habit that aligns with well-known author Stephen R. Covey's habit four in his popular book, <u>The Seven Habits of Highly Effective People</u>. This habit emphasizes the principle of mutual benefit.

So, what can you do to benefit the life of another? May I suggest speaking a thoughtful word to direct a person's destiny; contributing to a person's college fund; or organizing a community recycling day? Make it a habit to live wealthy. This is the power of giving your all.

> **"You may not ever know what you can become until you try to become it. Trying moves you that much closer to becoming."**

Another habit to keep is to live healthy. Living healthy means eating the right food and living a lifestyle that is worth living. There is an abundance of evidence that proves that unhealthy eating habits can cost you your life. Research has shown that some foods that we consume contribute to diseases such as high blood pressure, stroke, some cancers, heart disease, high cholesterol, and osteoporosis. I am not a medical doctor. However, I know how good my body feels when I live healthy by eating healthy foods; exercising; and having the right mind-set. I do not want my body to be at "dis-ease" and wreak with pain.

If it takes only 21 days to develop a habit, consider the habit to live healthy. This habit could affect the rest of your life. Give it your all. What do you have to lose? What do you have to gain? Living wealthy and living healthy are two good habits to keep. This is the power of giving your all.

## ∞ 15 ∞

# Plan 4 Legacy = 100%

| A | B | C | D | E | F | G | H | I | J | K | L | M | N | O | P | Q | R | S | T | U | V | W | X | Y | Z |
|---|---|---|---|---|---|---|---|---|---|---|---|---|---|---|---|---|---|---|---|---|---|---|---|---|---|
| 1 | 2 | 3 | 4 | 5 | 6 | 7 | 8 | 9 | 10 | 11 | 12 | 13 | 14 | 15 | 16 | 17 | 18 | 19 | 20 | 21 | 22 | 23 | 24 | 25 | 26 |

What will you do today that will shape your legacy for tomorrow?

When I think of legacy, Bill Gates comes to mind. His full legacy is yet to be seen. However, thus far he has made his mark. He has shaped a legacy of his own that extends to all points of the globe. How many lives will your legacy touch?

In 1968, while most teenagers were playing around in the neighborhood, Bill Gates was programming computers at the early age of thirteen. He probably was not thinking about legacy. But, today he is one of the richest persons in the world. In his junior year, he dropped out of Harvard and leaped into forming Microsoft Corporation in 1975. In 2007, Microsoft® grossed over $51 billion, and in 2009, Gates's personal net worth exceeded $40 billion. Now, that's a leap of faith. His vision for Microsoft® included a computer on every office desk and in every home. Wow! His legacy is constantly being shaped, every day.

Alfred Nobel is another person who comes to mind when I think of legacy. The famed chemist and inventor received over 350 patents for various inventions, but he is most widely known for his development of dynamite. Its original purpose was for improving the construction of tunnels, canals, and other related structures. Others used his invention for harm, particularly in war.

Alfred Nobel wanted his legacy to be positive and profound. Thus, he recorded in his will:

> The whole of my remaining realizable estate shall be dealt with in the following way: the capital, invested in safe securities by my executors, shall constitute a fund, the interest on which shall be annually distributed in the form of prizes to those who, during the preceding year, shall have conferred the greatest benefit on mankind. The said interest shall be divided into five equal parts, which shall be apportioned as follows: one part to the person who shall have made the most important discovery or invention within the field of physics; one part to the person who shall have made the most important chemical discovery or improvement; one part to the person who shall have made the most important discovery within the domain of physiology or medicine; one part to the person who shall

have produced in the field of literature the most outstanding work in an ideal direction; and one part to the person who shall have done the most or the best work for fraternity between nations, for the abolition or reduction of standing armies and for the holding and promotion of peace congresses.

Alfred Nobel died in 1896, but his legacy continues in the form of the most recognizable Nobel Peace Prize. He planned for legacy.

> "When my father departed this life, he left behind a great legacy. One of the things he left behind for me is a positive principle. Affectionately known as Mr. Bongo, he would constantly say and model to me that, whenever you leave a place, you should leave it in a better condition than you found it."

Just what is a legacy? It depends on context. In its simplest terms, a legacy is something that is left to someone else or an inheritance. When my father departed this life, he left behind a great legacy. One of the things he left behind for me is a positive principle. Affectionately known as Mr. Bongo, he would constantly say and model to me that, whenever you leave a place, you should leave it in a better condition than you found it. I inherited this great principle which helps to guide my actions today. I <u>will</u> make a place better than I found it. I want someone to know that there was someone present and accounted for. What do you will to do?

What type of legacy are you leaving behind at home; on your job; in your community; at your place of worship? Whatever you do, give it your all. Make your mark! Plan for legacy!

## ∞ 16 ∞
## Problems? = 100%

| A | B | C | D | E | F | G | H | I | J | K | L | M | N | O | P | Q | R | S | T | U | V | W | X | Y | Z |
|---|---|---|---|---|---|---|---|---|---|---|---|---|---|---|---|---|---|---|---|---|---|---|---|---|---|
| 1 | 2 | 3 | 4 | 5 | 6 | 7 | 8 | 9 | 10 | 11 | 12 | 13 | 14 | 15 | 16 | 17 | 18 | 19 | 20 | 21 | 22 | 23 | 24 | 25 | 26 |

Some people wait for opportunity to knock. The problem is: opportunity rarely knocks on the doors of idleness. Identify and solve people's problems and opportunity will knock your door off its hinges. Problems can be profitable. You can increase your income by identifying and solving problems. Ironically, as a matter of fact, problems can lead to an enriched life.

Consider the problem that Dr. Patricia Bath, African-American ophthalmologist and inventor, solved. By solving one problem, she solved many.

Allow me to explain, with an example that affected me personally. As a youngster, I was involved in an accident while playing baseball with a plastic bat and rocks. You are right. I should have known better. While throwing my last pitch of the day, a piece of gravel from the hole in the top of the bat was launched into my eye. I spent weeks recovering in a hospital. A few years later, a cataract developed on my eye. My blurred vision caused many problems. I did not see the twinkle in the stars for many years. My learning was hindered. My social life suffered as well. From a distance, I could not distinguish one person from the other. Glasses gave me a headache so I avoided wearing them and found ways to compensate. This thorn bothered me throughout high school and college. However, little did I know, someone was working on solving my problem.

> "The problem you solve today could create your path to prosperity, tomorrow."

In 1988, Dr. Bath became the first African-American female doctor to patent a medical invention when she developed the Laserphaco Probe. This device removed cataracts more accurately, safely, and painlessly than other devices then used for this purpose. In 1996, I was a recipient of the benefits of this device. Dr. Bath solved my problem when a doctor used this device to safely and painlessly remove my cataract. I rejoiced when I was able to see the stars in the sky. No doubt, others rejoiced too, when Dr. Bath invented another device which enabled doctors to restore sight to people who had been blind for many years. Dr. Bath identified problems and solved them. She has spent years giving her all to solve problems related to ophthalmology.

Solve people's problems. Improve their lives. It may take some time, but it will be worth trying. The problem you solve today could create your path to prosperity tomorrow. Got problems? Problems produce opportunities. You may have the solution inside of you. Give it out. This is the power of giving your all.

## ∞ 17 ∞
# Develop U = 100%

| A | B | C | D | E | F | G | H | I | J | K | L | M | N | O | P | Q | R | S | T | U | V | W | X | Y | Z |
|---|---|---|---|---|---|---|---|---|---|---|---|---|---|---|---|---|---|---|---|---|---|---|---|---|---|
| 1 | 2 | 3 | 4 | 5 | 6 | 7 | 8 | 9 | 10 | 11 | 12 | 13 | 14 | 15 | 16 | 17 | 18 | 19 | 20 | 21 | 22 | 23 | 24 | 25 | 26 |

You can develop you. You can deter you, too. You decide which you that you want to be. Being too critical of yourself and others will ultimately cloud your thinking of seeing the best ideas for being the best that you can be. You are human, mistakes will happen, but be careful not to promote them. What do I mean? Uncontrolled mistakes can become the hallmark of your life and not move you very far along at all. But, learning from a mistake is progress. That's developing you. So get going. Do something. The person who never does anything can be assured of one thing – failure.

Consider the challenges and triumphs of the great heavyweight boxer, George Foreman. He has developed himself from being a troublemaker as a youth to becoming an Olympic boxing champion; from undergoing four divorces to becoming a devoted family man with a marriage that has lasted for over 25 years; from a being criticized fighter to becoming a World Heavyweight Champion; from moving from a knock-out decision defeat to becoming a power-packed preacher; from being a defeated boxer to becoming a World Heavyweight Champion, again, at the age of 44.

George Foreman's life story is inspiring to anyone who has faced challenges. That includes all of us. He captures what "develop u" really means — namely, defeating defeats and overcoming obstacles.

To date, George Foreman continues to develop himself. He is a superb salesman. He has earned millions from packaging promotional infomercials for the George Foreman Lean Mean Grilling Machine and for Meineke® Car Care Centers. Additionally, he has marketed environmentally safe cleaning products, personal care products, health shakes, shoes for diabetics, and a big-and-tall men's clothing line. Furthermore, he is an accomplished author and a restaurant franchise owner. George continues to develop himself. What about you?

> "Your past is over. Are you over your past? Determine in your heart that you will not allow past failures and disappointments to destroy your future. Begin to develop you."

You can develop you. I believe that one of the principles of success that has propelled George Foreman is the ability to forget the past and set your sight on the future. George Foreman had plenty of adversity and struggle in his past, enough to knock most people down and out.

Your past is over. Are you over your past? Determine in your heart that you will not allow past failures and disappointments to destroy your future. Begin to develop you. Determine what you want to do. Begin to do it. Forget the naysayers. The naysayers are your "past people."

Dr. Mike Murdock, author of <u>The Uncommon Leader – 31 Keys for Unlocking Your Greatness</u>, and dynamic speaker and preacher, puts it this way: "God never reads your diary. Your past is over. Act like it. Talk like it. Live like it. Your best days are ahead of you." Dr. Murdock continues, by saying: "Make tomorrow bigger than yesterday."

Give your all and "develop u." You can do it. What do you have to lose, your future? Your future <u>is</u> at stake. Develop you and become a better you. This is the power of giving your all.

## ∞ 18 ∞
# Why Hope? = 100%

| A | B | C | D | E | F | G | H | I | J | K | L | M | N | O | P | Q | R | S | T | U | V | W | X | Y | Z |
|---|---|---|---|---|---|---|---|---|---|---|---|---|---|---|---|---|---|---|---|---|---|---|---|---|---|
| 1 | 2 | 3 | 4 | 5 | 6 | 7 | 8 | 9 | 10 | 11 | 12 | 13 | 14 | 15 | 16 | 17 | 18 | 19 | 20 | 21 | 22 | 23 | 24 | 25 | 26 |

A live dog is better than a dead lion. This profound truth is found in the Bible. What does it mean? This means, regardless of your condition, as long as you are alive, there is hope. You still have a chance. You are not out. However, there is no hope in the grave. In the grave, our labors cease to be.

Is there something you still want to do in life? Of course there is. If you are reading this book, there's a good chance that you can do it. There is hope. You can still fulfill your assignment. Pope John XXIII once said, "Consult not your fears but your hopes and dreams. Think not about your frustrations, but about your unfulfilled potential. Concern yourself not with what you tried and failed in, but with what is still possible for you to do."

Why hope? Hope keeps us going. Hope helps define our existence. I capture hope this way: It's a desire to have something happen and believing, because of some reason, that it will. Hope is a precursor for faith. Hope helps you think about results. Faith and works get you the results.

> "Hope helps you think about results. Faith and works get you the results."

Hope reminds me of the late, accomplished coach Jimmy Valvano. Most people knew him as the charismatic coach, Jimmy V, who led his N.C. State University basketball team to a surprising upset victory over the number-one seeded and highly favored University of Houston Cougars in the 1983 National Championship game. It was one of the most dramatic wins in college basketball history. The hope and faith of Jimmy V and his team were quite visible.

However, Jimmy Valvano was more than a coach. As a young teenager, he wrote his goals on an index card and actively pursued and accomplished them. He continued this practice in his adult life as well. He became a motivational speaker, authored three books, hosted weekly television and radio broadcasts, started a successful business, and served as an award-winning sports commentator. He was a family man with a zest for life. Jamie Valvano Howard, his middle daughter, wrote, "He certainly loved the limelight, but he also hoped that others would learn from the way in which he lived life. He wanted to matter to someone and to everyone."

At the young age of 47, Jimmy Valvano's life was ended due to bone cancer, on April 28, 1993. But his legacy of life continues through his family and The Jimmy V Foundation for Cancer Research. His foundation embodies the courage to find hope in the face of despair.

Why hope? Hope gives you the confidence that life is worth living. Hope and faith are close kin. Hope puts you on the path to faith. Hope encourages you to give your all with the expectation that something good is going to happen. Hope on and give it all that you've got. This is the power of giving your all.

## ∞ 19 ∞

# Get Giving = 100%

| A | B | C | D | E | F | G | H | I | J | K | L | M | N | O | P | Q | R | S | T | U | V | W | X | Y | Z |
|---|---|---|---|---|---|---|---|---|---|---|---|---|---|---|---|---|---|---|---|---|---|---|---|---|---|
| | | | | | | | | | | 1 | 1 | 1 | 1 | 1 | 1 | 1 | 1 | 1 | 2 | 2 | 2 | 2 | 2 | 2 | 2 |
| 1 | 2 | 3 | 4 | 5 | 6 | 7 | 8 | 9 | 0 | 1 | 2 | 3 | 4 | 5 | 6 | 7 | 8 | 9 | 0 | 1 | 2 | 3 | 4 | 5 | 6 |

Don't you just love it when you get something for free? You go to a department store or grocery store and they are giving out free samples of some of their products. They are giving with an end in mind. They are trying to motivate you to buy the product or better still, become a repeat customer. Sometimes, you will even circle back around for seconds and thirds. You feel great to receive the product without any cost to you. Do you feel equally as great when you are doing the giving?

Andrew Carnegie was feeling at his best when he was doing the giving. As a matter of fact, by 1919, at the time of his death, as a philanthropist he had given over $350,000,000 to causes promoting the advancement of knowledge and understanding. Given today's value, that would be over $4.0 billion. His endowment today is at an estimated value of over $3.0 billion. How did he amass so much wealth and then give most of it away? The answer is found in his thinking.

Andrew Carnegie believed that the rich should use their wealth to help enrich society. Carnegie went from humble beginnings to becoming a huge giver. His jobs included: factory worker, bill logger, messenger boy, and telegraph factory worker, before he amassed his wealth. Eventually, he formed Pittsburgh's Carnegie Steel Company, which later became US Steel. As noted in the Bible, despise not small beginnings.

Carnegie also invested in the lucrative railroad industry at the time and its related industries such as iron, bridges, and rails. This investment laid the foundation for his wealth. Specifically, his formula for wealth was a three-step approach. First, spend the first third of your life obtaining all of the education that you can get. Secondly, spend the next third earning all of the money you can. The third and final step is to give all of your money away for worthwhile causes. What a plan! Basically, Andrew Carnegie followed this plan and he's still giving through his foundations. He used his wealth to promote libraries, schools, world peace, and scientific research.

> "You feel great to receive ...without any cost to you. Do you feel equally as great when you are doing the giving?"

The message from Carnegie's life is: "Get Giving." That's right, you need to get giving. You can start in your home or local community. Get giving to the good in your community. You may say, there's no good in my community; you don't know where I live. Well, your charge is to *create* the good in your community.

For example, my wife implemented a splendid idea for giving. We had a yard sale whereby we donated a portion of the profits to a charity. We advertised in our local community and informed family and friends via email. The yard sale was a great success. Also, it presented an opportunity to teach our young daughters about caring for others; being responsible; and working as a team for a worthwhile cause. Get giving. You can do it. This is the power of giving your all.

## ∞ 20 ∞

## Speak 2 Win = 100%

| A | B | C | D | E | F | G | H | I | J | K | L | M | N | O | P | Q | R | S | T | U | V | W | X | Y | Z |
|---|---|---|---|---|---|---|---|---|---|---|---|---|---|---|---|---|---|---|---|---|---|---|---|---|---|
|   |   |   |   |   |   |   |   |   |   | 1 | 1 | 1 | 1 | 1 | 1 | 1 | 1 | 1 | 2 | 2 | 2 | 2 | 2 | 2 | 2 |
| 1 | 2 | 3 | 4 | 5 | 6 | 7 | 8 | 9 | 0 | 1 | 2 | 3 | 4 | 5 | 6 | 7 | 8 | 9 | 0 | 1 | 2 | 3 | 4 | 5 | 6 |

You can't see the spoken word. You can't hear the written word. Yet, you can experience the manifestation of the word by hearing it; speaking it; and doing it. You must believe that the words you speak have creative power!

What are you creating with your words?

The old adage, "Sticks and stones may break my bones, but words will never hurt me" is so very far from the truth. You can speak words that cause you to lose in life – that hurts. Or you can speak to win. Words can lift us up or tear us down. They can make us cry or make us laugh. The Bible says, "Death and life are in the power of the tongue." What a powerful and bold truth.

We make the choice to live or die by our words. I believe that there is a powerful connection between the words we speak and the results we get. No doubt, you can probably recall countless times whereby persons have chosen to use what I call "death words" and it has been to their detriment and hastened their demise. This unnecessary outcome is evident in all walks of life and at various levels of society. Why choose words that can bring death to your dreams and goals, and cause you to lose, when you can speak to win? Sometimes it is not wise to say what you think, but it *is* wise to think about what you say.

> ## "If you want to be on top in life, begin at the bottom of your nose."

What are you thinking, regarding your words? Are you saying words that can make an everlasting change in your life? What will you tell yourself that will cause you to give your all? I encourage you to speak life. As an educator, whenever I have to deal with a conflict, oftentimes I find that verbal communication is at the root of the problem.

So I encourage you to speak words that inspire and not insult. Speak words that build up and not break down. Speak words that are positive and not pugnacious. Charles Capps, a retired farmer and dynamic preacher, says, "The words you speak will either put you over in life or hold you in bondage." This is the bottom line. If you want to be on top in life, begin at the bottom of your nose.

Words determine destiny. Oftentimes, we say things to ourselves and others not realizing the imprint that is made. I decided to pursue a graduate degree based on the words of a mentor. Words speak to eternity. Speak your words, carefully.

Some physicians say that it takes about 100 muscles for humans to use in order to speak. Exercise the power in your mouth. Make your words count. Speak life. Choose to live – speak to win. This is the power of giving your all.

## ∞ 21 ∞
# 100% Determined = 100%

| A | B | C | D | E | F | G | H | I | J | K | L | M | N | O | P | Q | R | S | T | U | V | W | X | Y | Z |
|---|---|---|---|---|---|---|---|---|---|---|---|---|---|---|---|---|---|---|---|---|---|---|---|---|---|
|   |   |   |   |   |   |   |   |   | 1 | 1 | 1 | 1 | 1 | 1 | 1 | 1 | 1 | 1 | 2 | 2 | 2 | 2 | 2 | 2 | 2 |
| 1 | 2 | 3 | 4 | 5 | 6 | 7 | 8 | 9 | 0 | 1 | 2 | 3 | 4 | 5 | 6 | 7 | 8 | 9 | 0 | 1 | 2 | 3 | 4 | 5 | 6 |

The wings of determination soar against all odds. The year was 1892. A 100% determined pilot was born. Determination was birthed in this little Black girl from Texas. She was one of six children. Bessie Coleman's mother was Black and her father was Native American. Her parents could not read, nor write; but, they were hard workers. She attended segregated schools. In the midst of denial and need, Bessie Coleman excelled in math.

Responsibility breeds self-confidence. Bessie Coleman's parents decided to split up while she was still a child. She began assuming adult-like tasks by taking care of her younger siblings. Regardless of the mounting obstacles, Bessie Coleman wanted to do something special with her life. One of her three brothers provided the spark. Drawing from his service in the U.S. Army, he commented to Bessie that she would never fly like the women in France. At that point, Bessie Coleman's calling was clear. She wanted to fly.

The significant obstacles to her doing so began early on in her quest for pilot training and increased over time. Bessie sought out several flying schools, but none would teach her to fly. She was a woman and Black.

Given the advice of a Black businessman, she decided to obtain her pilot's license in France, where more opportunities awaited Blacks and women. Bessie worked hard as a manicurist and domestic to save enough money to travel to France. Also, she took the time and made the effort to learn French. In 1920, at the age of 28, the 100% determined, Bessie Coleman began her long journey to France, sailing on the *S. S. Imparator*. While in France, again she faced rejection as she tried to apply to flight school. Finally, her goal of flying began to take off when the Aviation School of the Caudron Brothers enrolled her in their famous flight school. She fought through the rough and tough training of becoming a pilot and even witnessed the death of a fellow student. But, Bessie Coleman was 100% determined. On June 15, 1921, Bessie Coleman became the first Black woman to receive a pilot's license.

> **"The wings of determination soar against all odds."**

Obstacles and opportunities continued to be in Bessie's path. Soon after receiving her pilot's license,

Coleman returned to the United States to do air shows. There were few opportunities to do anything else. But, still 100% determined, she expanded her goal to open her own flight school. She achieved celebrity status, lectured and taught about aviation, earned enough money to purchase her first airplane, and was well on her way to her next goal. However, tragedy struck on April 29, 1926. While en route to an air show, a wrench that was left on the floor of the airplane got stuck in the gear shaft, causing the plane to accelerate and nosedive to the ground.

Bessie Coleman's determination influenced thousands of people – Black and white. In 1929, William J. Powell, a Black businessman, founded the Bessie Coleman Aero Club, located in Chicago.

> "Being determined can encourage others around you. People are drawn towards winners. Accomplishments welcome those who dare to accomplish. Be 100% determined and favor will follow you."

I think of another woman when I think about determination. That woman is Kinta Jones. She is my wife. Whatever she is tasked to do, she becomes 100% determined to see it done. Rather than accepting excuses, she seeks resources. Instead of giving in to obstacles, she finds opportunities. Rather than throwing in the towel, she takes the towel to remove the sweat from her brow and keeps on moving towards the goal.

Being determined can encourage others around you. People are drawn towards winners. Accomplishments welcome those who dare to accomplish. Be 100% determined and favor will follow you. This is the power of giving your all.

## ∞ 22 ∞
# Higher & Above = 100%

| A | B | C | D | E | F | G | H | I | J | K | L | M | N | O | P | Q | R | S | T | U | V | W | X | Y | Z |
|---|---|---|---|---|---|---|---|---|---|---|---|---|---|---|---|---|---|---|---|---|---|---|---|---|---|
|   |   |   |   |   |   |   |   |   |   | 1 | 1 | 1 | 1 | 1 | 1 | 1 | 1 | 1 | 2 | 2 | 2 | 2 | 2 | 2 | 2 |
| 1 | 2 | 3 | 4 | 5 | 6 | 7 | 8 | 9 | 0 | 1 | 2 | 3 | 4 | 5 | 6 | 7 | 8 | 9 | 0 | 1 | 2 | 3 | 4 | 5 | 6 |

An attitude could ground you and keep you from going higher and moving above your circumstances. What does this mean? I'm glad you asked. I was on an airplane going to Chicago en route to Beijing, China. A passenger was searching for an overhead bin to secure his carry-on luggage. This lasted for only a few minutes. A flight attendant assisted him by alerting him to a vacant bin, several seats away from where he was seated. The passenger said, "Thank you." The flight attendant responded with a smile, saying, "I'm just trying to be helpful."

Okay, now we are ready for take-off, to go higher and above. But the story doesn't end here. It is just beginning. Surprisingly, the passenger rudely recanted, "Yeah, after you watched me struggle for 20 minutes." His remark was definitely unwarranted. This passenger had an attitude – a bad one. As a result, the flight attendant's friendly countenance changed to that of a frown. However, he continued to do his job. The flight attendant responded to a bad attitude with a professional promise. He firmly stated, "Sir, if you have an attitude, you're off the plane." The bad attitude was about to ground the passenger.

Is your attitude keeping you from taking off; launching your dreams and ideas; and reaching your full potential? You've heard the saying, "Your attitude could determine your altitude." This is true, particularly in this story, figuratively and literally. The proper attitude allowed the passenger to go higher and above and get to his destination.

> **"Is your attitude keeping you from taking off; launching your dreams and ideas; and reaching your full potential?"**

One critical observation I noticed during the exchange between the flight attendant and the passenger is that authority and instruction can change a person's attitude. In essence, the flight attendant was speaking from a position of authority. The instruction he gave clearly indicated what the outcome would be if the passenger spoke or did something else indicative of a bad attitude. The authority and instruction in those ten spoken words changed the passenger's attitude. Some would argue that his actions were changed, not his attitude. Nevertheless, the flight attendant got the desired results.

This leads us to an important question; namely: Who are you being instructed by? Is the person an authority on the subject? Will the instruction promote you in going higher and above your circumstances? Your attitude will tend to take shape by the instruction and instructor you take heed to. You can choose to surround yourself with people to help you develop your attitude. The choice is yours to make. Don't be grounded! Don't delay the flight! Go higher and above. This is the power of giving your all.

## ∞ 23 ∞
# No "I" in Team = 100%

| A | B | C | D | E | F | G | H | I | J | K | L | M | N | O | P | Q | R | S | T | U | V | W | X | Y | Z |
|---|---|---|---|---|---|---|---|---|---|---|---|---|---|---|---|---|---|---|---|---|---|---|---|---|---|
| 1 | 2 | 3 | 4 | 5 | 6 | 7 | 8 | 9 | 10 | 11 | 12 | 13 | 14 | 15 | 16 | 17 | 18 | 19 | 20 | 21 | 22 | 23 | 24 | 25 | 26 |

By most accounts, we won some games that we should have lost. I'm talking about my high school basketball team. I believe we won because of our collective passion and desire as a team to do so. Yeah, there's no "i" in team, but there is an "i" in passion and desire. Passion and desire will cause you to find a way to win. Passion and desire will cause you to excel beyond the expectations of others. Just ask Larry Jordan, older brother of legendary basketball player, Michael Jordan. Larry and I played intramural basketball together in college. No doubt, Larry is a winner and competitor. It has been said that Michael got his competitive edge from Larry.

What about the game of life? I believe passion and desire make a great team that can help you win in life. Winning in life is about living a productive and abundant life. It's about living with purpose. It's about making a difference in the lives of others. But unlike the game of basketball, winning in life does not mean that someone has to lose.

Passion and desire create the enthusiasm for what you do in life. What would happen if you ratcheted up your passion and desire regarding your job performance at work? Would the bottom line increase? Who would benefit? How might your family life be impacted if you showed more enthusiasm for your role as a parent? Maintaining your passion and a strong desire for what you do will prompt other people around you to get excited about your cause and support your efforts. They will see the worthiness of your cause and be compelled to contribute. Let your passion show and mediocrity will be far from you.

> "Yeah, there's no "i" in team, but there is an "i" in passion and desire. Passion and desire will cause you to find a way to win. Passion and desire will cause you to excel beyond the expectations of others."

What are you most passionate about? What do you desire to do most of all? These are two important questions to be answered on the road to becoming a better you. Take the time to find out what really makes you tick. It could be the spark that inspires you and others, too.

Another important question to answer is: Who's on your winning team? There's no way Michael Jordan could have won six NBA championships without his teammates. Similarly, there is no way for you to win in life without the help of others. We are designed and created to be relational human beings. The *Message Bible* puts it this way: "It's better to have a partner than to go it alone. Share the work, share the wealth. And if one falls down, the other helps, but if there's no one to help, tough!" Also, it says: "By yourself you're unprotected. With a friend you can face the worst. Can you round up a third? A three-stranded rope isn't easily snapped." So, find your passion and desire. Then, develop your team. Michael Jordan said, "There's an "i" in win." I believe you can win in life. This is the power of giving your all.

## ∞ 24 ∞
# U Begin and End = 100%

| A | B | C | D | E | F | G | H | I | J | K | L | M | N | O | P | Q | R | S | T | U | V | W | X | Y | Z |
|---|---|---|---|---|---|---|---|---|---|---|---|---|---|---|---|---|---|---|---|---|---|---|---|---|---|
| 1 | 2 | 3 | 4 | 5 | 6 | 7 | 8 | 9 | 10 | 11 | 12 | 13 | 14 | 15 | 16 | 17 | 18 | 19 | 20 | 21 | 22 | 23 | 24 | 25 | 26 |

Please, don't quit! Far too many people begin to achieve a goal or do a project and give up on their expected end. I don't think many people actually plan to quit high school, college, or a job. They don't sit down, do research, and write out strategies and plans to quit. However, if you do, you should begin with the end in mind. I believe, if you begin it, you can end it.

A report from America's Promise Alliance and the Bill & Melinda Gates Foundation indicated that approximately 1.2 million students drop out of high school each year. This equates to a dropout rate of about 30 percent. Even more alarming is the dropout rate among African Americans and Latinos, which is nearly 50 percent. Let's examine the next level, college. Of the vast number of students who attend a four-year college or university expecting to earn a degree, only 40 to 50 percent of them actually do so. Finally, how many people actually quit their job? The U.S. Bureau of Labor Statistics, reports that there are nearly 116 million people employed by private companies. On average, about 20 percent will quit their jobs each year.

You can begin and end. You can finish the race, cross the finish line, and receive the prize. As I think about these three venues – high school, college, and the workplace, I see a common thread that supports the success level at each turn. That common thread is relationships. High schools with high graduation rates have adults committed to individual students who may be at risk of failing and dropping out. Colleges and universities understand the importance of caring advisors who guide students through the post-secondary process and stick it out to the end. They understand that an expected end is more important than high enrollment. Companies with low turnover rates know that the persons in charge of others are the main key to promoting staying power for employees. Many reports indicate that bad bosses are the number one cause of employee turnover. People relate to people.

When you begin and end, you have a resolve to finish what you start. This requires you to be steadfast, creative, reflective, competent, skilled, and able to get along with others. Reading, writing, and arithmetic will get you to where you want to go, but relationships will help you to stay and grow. This is the power of giving your all.

Develop your relationship skills. Take the time to get to know people. As long as you are here on the earth, people will be here, too. Actually, you begin and end with relationships. Don't quit! Get someone to help you begin and end. This is the power of giving your all.

## ∞ 25 ∞
## "Ganas" & Stand = 100%

| A | B | C | D | E | F | G | H | I | J | K | L | M | N | O | P | Q | R | S | T | U | V | W | X | Y | Z |
|---|---|---|---|---|---|---|---|---|---|---|---|---|---|---|---|---|---|---|---|---|---|---|---|---|---|
| 1 | 2 | 3 | 4 | 5 | 6 | 7 | 8 | 9 | 10 | 11 | 12 | 13 | 14 | 15 | 16 | 17 | 18 | 19 | 20 | 21 | 22 | 23 | 24 | 25 | 26 |

Got ganas? "Ganas" is a Spanish word meaning the urge to succeed. If you were ever touched by the amazing teaching gift of Jaime Escalante, you got ganas. Dr. Escalante once commented, "You don't count how many times you are on the floor, you count how many times you get up." – March 4, 2010. Let me explain.

When adversity rises up in your life, don't cower down, it may be your ticket to advancement. Such is the story of the late Jaime Escalante. Although he taught mathematics and physics in his native country of Bolivia for 14 years, he later had to perform menial jobs and face many challenges because of not knowing the English language when he moved to the United States in 1964. However, he stood up to the challenges and, a decade later, he delivered on his passion to teach when he was hired at Garfield High School in Los Angeles, California.

The challenges didn't stop there, they continued. Garfield High School was the home to students that some deemed "unteachable" and the school's accreditation was in jeopardy. Again, Jaime Escalante stood and delivered.

## 100 Percent: The Power of Giving Your All

In 1979, he taught his first calculus class. Two years later, 14 of his 15 students passed the advanced placement (AP) calculus exam administered by the Educational Testing Service (ETS). One year later, this same governing body questioned the scores of the 18 students who had passed the very challenging AP calculus exam because they all missed item number six with the same error. Jaime Escalante contended that the students were being discriminated against because they were Hispanic and from a disadvantaged school. Most of the students re-took the test and they all passed, again. This adversity led to Escalante's achieving advancement.

> "You can excel. You can succeed. Take a stand and deliver. Follow the path of your passion. Seek to meet the needs of others. You got ganas?"

Escalante had ganas. His urge to succeed overcame the adversity in his life and the lives of his students. In 1988, the well-known Washington Post reporter, Jay Mathews, released a book, *Escalante: The Best Teacher in America*. Later, the film "Stand and Deliver" was a huge success as it captured the challenges and successes of Escalante's life and career. Escalante continued to experience great success as his students continued to excel in math and learning.

The question for you is – Got ganas? What do you want to excel in? What are you willing to stand for? Dr. Martin Luther King, Jr. once said, "The ultimate measure of a man is not where he stands in moments of comfort and convenience, but where he stands at times of challenge and controversy."

You can excel. You can succeed. Take a stand and deliver. Follow the path of your passion. Seek to meet the needs of others. You got ganas? Or, you got ganas. Ganas and stand – this is the power of giving your all.

## ∞ 26 ∞
# Academics Pay = 100%

| A | B | C | D | E | F | G | H | I | J | K | L | M | N | O | P | Q | R | S | T | U | V | W | X | Y | Z |
|---|---|---|---|---|---|---|---|---|---|---|---|---|---|---|---|---|---|---|---|---|---|---|---|---|---|
|   |   |   |   |   |   |   |   |   |   | 1 | 1 | 1 | 1 | 1 | 1 | 1 | 1 | 1 | 2 | 2 | 2 | 2 | 2 | 2 | 2 |
| 1 | 2 | 3 | 4 | 5 | 6 | 7 | 8 | 9 | 0 | 1 | 2 | 3 | 4 | 5 | 6 | 7 | 8 | 9 | 0 | 1 | 2 | 3 | 4 | 5 | 6 |

Here is a $54,000 question. Are you going to begin and end? I mean, are you going to finish what you start? Did you know, according to the U.S. Labor Department, in 2009, workers with a bachelor's degree earned 54 percent more money on average than those who attended college, but didn't finish? Now, you know.

Let's put this equation in perspective. For example, if you have college credits without the degree and earn $100,000 per year, you could potentially be making $154,000 with the degree. What could you do with an additional $54,000? Better still, what could you do with an extra quarter of a million dollars, over a five-year period?

Data from the US Census Bureau indicate that lifetime earnings generally soar with educational attainment. For example, based on 1999 dollars, on average a high school graduate can expect to earn about $1.2 million during one's lifetime of earnings. A person with a bachelor's degree will earn almost double ($2.1 million) that of a person with a high school diploma. A master's degree will net you about $2.5 million. These lifetime earnings generally increase over time.

Let's look at earnings at a level we are more accustomed to. In 2009, the Bureau of Labor Statistics reported that the median weekly earnings of a person with a high school diploma was $638 or a monthly income of about $2,552. As expected, income increases with educational attainment. Workers with a bachelor's degree can expect a median weekly income of $1,121, and a master's degree or professional degree will increase that income even more. The highest-earning 10 percent of workers with advanced degrees earned about $3,342 or more per week for males and $2,156 for females.

Education pays in more ways than one. In 2008, the unemployment rate among persons without a high school diploma was 9.0 percent. Get a high school diploma and the unemployment rate drops to 5.7 percent. A bachelor's degree rendered an unemployment rate of 2.8 percent. As technology and innovation continue to bring the world closer together, competition for jobs will increase. Education attainment could be the difference between being employed and being unemployed.

> "Saying no to learning is like saving your life's earnings in a shoe box. Your capacity to save is limited to the size of the box."

The bottom line is this: The more you learn, the more your potential to earn. Certainly, there are a few exceptions – Bill Gates dropped out of college, but he didn't stop learning. He dropped into Microsoft. I think you know the rest of his story.

My message is take advantage of every opportunity to learn and learn with gladness. Saying no to learning is like saving your life's earnings in a shoe box. Your capacity to save is limited to the size of the box. Be a lifelong learner. Academics pay. A lifelong learner is a lifelong earner. Commit to learning. This is the power of giving your all.

## ∞ 27 ∞
## Y Dn't Qt = 100%

| A | B | C | D | E | F | G | H | I | J | K | L | M | N | O | P | Q | R | S | T | U | V | W | X | Y | Z |
|---|---|---|---|---|---|---|---|---|---|---|---|---|---|---|---|---|---|---|---|---|---|---|---|---|---|
| 1 | 2 | 3 | 4 | 5 | 6 | 7 | 8 | 9 | 10 | 11 | 12 | 13 | 14 | 15 | 16 | 17 | 18 | 19 | 20 | 21 | 22 | 23 | 24 | 25 | 26 |

When pursuing your goals, all the pieces of the puzzle may not be visible. Still, you don't quit. Keep going. You can do it. You still have to see it done. See yourself doing what you envisioned to do. You don't quit.

For some people, the word "no" becomes their final destination. In the words of Dr. Michael Freeman, "'No' today does not [have to] mean 'no' tomorrow." Think forward.

I encourage you to keep trying, don't give up, don't quit. View "no" as a "**new opportunity**" to try again. Stay in the game!

One difference between a person who quits and one who continues is confidence. The confidence to continue in the face of adversity and challenge is very powerful and contagious. My pastor, A. Troy Harrison, once said, "Confidence acts like a magnet. It will draw to you whatever you are confident in." Confidence will help you to move past what you don't see. And, just because you don't see all of the details, it's not a reason to quit.

Consider the origins of two common household products – WD-40® and Formula 409®. WD-40® is put to work as a rust-prevention solvent and lubricant for thousands of uses. Its name is derived from the persistence of the inventor (Norm Larsen) who chose not to quit in his quest to develop a top-quality water-displacing formula. He achieved his desired results with the 40th solution, hence the name WD-40®. Similarly, it took 409 opportunities for the inventors (the Rouff brothers) of the Formula 409® cleaner to get it right. They could have chosen to quit at formula 109, but 300 more attempts later, they accomplished their goal and developed a high quality cleaner that takes no mess. They didn't quit.

> "Keep trying, don't give up, you don't quit. View "no" as a "<u>n</u>ew <u>o</u>pportunity" to try again."

Also, I'm reminded how watching others with the wrong intent can be detrimental to your progress. Ever wondered how or why some people get promoted? Watching others around you get promoted can encourage or discourage you. You decide what goes before courage. You can choose the "en" or the "dis." Choose the "en" crowd. You may not be aware or see what another person has done to get where they are. You may not know what they have done to position themselves for promotion. Yes, some people may be promoted ahead of you. However, you can still win. Your gifts and talents will make room for you. Continue to work with a spirit of excellence and strive to exceed the expectations and responsibilities of your job. You don't quit. Be encouraged, not discouraged.

Make sacrifices. Sacrifice precedes success. Jesse Duplantis, author of <u>The Everyday Visionary: Focus Your Thoughts, Change Your Life</u>, minister and "funny man," says, "I believe it with everything I am … you cannot have success without sacrifice." Make the sacrifice and succeed— you don't quit!

> "…when life knocks you to the ground with a left hook, you've got to do the right thing and get up."

Finally, when life knocks you to the ground with a left hook, you've got to do the right thing and get up. The ground is no place for a champion. There's a champion in you. You've got to get up. You don't quit (Y Dn't Qt), even if pieces to the puzzle are missing. This is the power of giving your all.

## ∞ 28 ∞
## Ever Advance = 100%

| A | B | C | D | E | F | G | H | I | J | K | L | M | N | O | P | Q | R | S | T | U | V | W | X | Y | Z |
|---|---|---|---|---|---|---|---|---|---|---|---|---|---|---|---|---|---|---|---|---|---|---|---|---|---|
| 1 | 2 | 3 | 4 | 5 | 6 | 7 | 8 | 9 | 10 | 11 | 12 | 13 | 14 | 15 | 16 | 17 | 18 | 19 | 20 | 21 | 22 | 23 | 24 | 25 | 26 |

Keep going. Keep growing. You get the picture? In 2009, I had the great pleasure of visiting the proud country of China. It was an awesome experience. One of my destinations included a prestigious middle school in Beijing. The school's emblem included the words "Ever Advancing." What a positive mantra! When I think about the phrase "ever advancing," several thoughts come to mind —challenge, change, excellence, new ideas, and high expectations.

Those who take on challenges put themselves in the position-and-set zone. They are positioned and set for promotion and progress. Challenges bring about new ideas and new insights. Take the challenge and ever advance.

Those who change are those who lead. Also, effective leaders create change. They continuously seek a better way. Change may often involve pain and resistance. However, one true test of change is the joy and silence of one-time critics.

Those who operate with the spirit of excellence attract top-notch people. Excellence is not for all. For some, even the very word makes them uncomfortable.

But, for those who embrace this ever-demanding cycle of continuous improvement, the rewards and by-products are overwhelmingly satisfying.

New ideas belong to those who question the status quo. They put the extra in front of the ordinary. New-idea thinkers are not afraid of ridicule or failure. While most people are thinking outside of the box, new-idea thinkers never see the box. Their thinking is totally different and genuinely new. Fresh thinking leads to fresh ideas.

Those who communicate high expectations see obstacles as opportunities; replace fear with faith; and pursue a goal with passion. High expectations keep you fresh and allow you to dream in technicolor.

> **"Keep going. Keep growing. You get the picture?"**

Ever advance. This is not only an excellent vision statement for a school. It is an excellent direction for a way of life. And if you are to advance, you must start in your mind. See yourself making progress every day; every month; every year. Ever advance. Grand rewards await you. This is the power of giving your all.

## ∞ 29 ∞
## Edify Daily = 100%

| A | B | C | D | E | F | G | H | I | J | K | L | M | N | O | P | Q | R | S | T | U | V | W | X | Y | Z |
|---|---|---|---|---|---|---|---|---|---|---|---|---|---|---|---|---|---|---|---|---|---|---|---|---|---|
| 1 | 2 | 3 | 4 | 5 | 6 | 7 | 8 | 9 | 10 | 11 | 12 | 13 | 14 | 15 | 16 | 17 | 18 | 19 | 20 | 21 | 22 | 23 | 24 | 25 | 26 |

The word "edification" is like a song that is at the very bottom of the music charts – you don't hear it too often. However, the practice of edification is a powerful principle that can produce exponential favor in your life. Mac Hammond, host of *The Winner's Way* broadcast, sought-after speaker, and minister says, "Edification is a fancy-sounding word, but it simply means to rebuild that which has been torn down."

Which leads me to ask the question: Who are you rebuilding? Are you taking the time to motivate and invest in someone else? Edification promotes advancement and productivity. When you edify another, you are guiding that person along a path that is narrow enough to stay focused on a desired goal and wide enough for others to travel along the side. Edification always helps. It never hinders.

Dr. Joe Louis Dudley, founder and CEO of Dudley Beauty Corporation, is the epitome of an enlightened man using the model of edification. Examining his upbringing and path to success gives us insight into why he makes it a priority to edify others. The Dudley household was quite crowded with Joe, his parents, grandfather, and ten siblings occupying a three-bedroom farmhouse in Aurora, North Carolina. He was held back twice by the time he reached the 11th grade; was labeled mentally retarded; and overcame a speech impediment. Many people had abysmal expectations for the young Joe Dudley. But, his mother edified him and encouraged him to prove them wrong.

Without a doubt, Joe Dudley exceeded all expectations. He made a promise to God that if He helped him make it, he would spend his life helping other people. He was well on his way by then. He graduated high school and earned a business administration degree from North Carolina A&T State University in Greensboro, North Carolina. I recall shaking his hand at a homecoming parade. His handshake and engaging smile were both genuine.

Dr. Dudley's father instilled in all of his children the legacy of working for oneself and becoming self-employed. Thus, while still in college, Joe Dudley invested $10 in Fuller Products and joined the company as a door-to-door salesman. Under the mentorship of Samuel B. Fuller, Joe Dudley would later learn the Fuller philosophy of sales and become an astute entrepreneur. In 1967, he founded Dudley Products. Today, Dudley Products produces more than 400 beauty agents, with annual revenue of more than $30 million.

Dr. Dudley seeks to edify others by having a personal goal of producing 250 millionaires. This goal was also the dream of S. B. Fuller, his mentor. Additionally, Dr. Dudley provides scholarships for students to attend college; donates to various charities; and serves as a role model for others wanting to succeed in the beauty business. Furthermore, in addition to manufacturing hair-care and beauty products, Dr. Dudley leads Dudley Cosmetology University, which teaches courses in five different languages. At the core of his work is the edification of others. How many people do you know who want to develop millionaires? Edification has brought about favor in Dr. Dudley's life.

> **"Edification promotes advancement and productivity. When you edify another, you are guiding that person along a path that is narrow enough to stay focused on a desired goal and wide enough for others to travel along the side. Edification always helps. It never hinders."**

Who will you edify today? The edification of another is choice driven. You must choose and plan to make edification a part of your life. Edify daily. There's something very special about edifying another person. It's a selfless act that renders great dividends in the lives of others. Not only are others blessed, but the blessing is multiplied in your life, too. Edify daily. This is the power of giving your all.

## ∞ 30 ∞
## Failure Is… = 100%

| A | B | C | D | E | F | G | H | I | J | K | L | M | N | O | P | Q | R | S | T | U | V | W | X | Y | Z |
|---|---|---|---|---|---|---|---|---|---|---|---|---|---|---|---|---|---|---|---|---|---|---|---|---|---|
| 1 | 2 | 3 | 4 | 5 | 6 | 7 | 8 | 9 | 10 | 11 | 12 | 13 | 14 | 15 | 16 | 17 | 18 | 19 | 20 | 21 | 22 | 23 | 24 | 25 | 26 |

Failure is an opportunity to learn how to succeed. This is what failure is to a winner, a champion, a never-give-upper. Some call failure the secret to success. I believe we are created to succeed. Check out these famous "failures."

> ➢ He missed the final shot in a high school basketball championship game. Yet, he holds the record for the most college basketball championships and is known as one of the winningest coaches of all-time – John Wooden.

> ➢ She was devastated by the death of her mother. After a divorce, she suffered from bouts of depression while raising her daughter as a single mother. However, she went from welfare to wealth when she imagined the first edition of the <u>Harry Potter</u> novel, while being delayed for hours on a train. Even then, she was rejected by 12

publishers before *Harry Potter* bombarded the bookshelves – J.K. Rowling.

> He was fired from his newspaper job and was told that he lacked imagination and had no original ideas – Walt Disney.

These are three prime examples of many persons that have risen from the ashes of failure.

> "Failure is not your final chapter. You can re-write the ending of your life's story if you hold the pen of determination and vision."

Failure is not your final chapter. You can re-write the ending of your life's story if you hold the pen of determination and vision. Do something! If you don't know what to do with your life, help someone else reach the top. You may be inspired along the way. All you need is one seed planted in your mind. It could be the start of something great! Without a vision; without a goal; without a determined destiny, people perish. Don't stagnate.

Always aspire to do great. Failure is not an option. Failure is not final. Failure is grotesquely overrated. Consider this. Three out of ten on a quiz may be a setback. But, three out of ten on the baseball diamond is a top-notch hitter. Find your place and win. You can succeed. This is the power of giving your all.

## ∞ 31 ∞

# Do It Now = 100%

| A | B | C | D | E | F | G | H | I | J | K | L | M | N | O | P | Q | R | S | T | U | V | W | X | Y | Z |
|---|---|---|---|---|---|---|---|---|---|---|---|---|---|---|---|---|---|---|---|---|---|---|---|---|---|
|   |   |   |   |   |   |   |   |   |   | 1 | 1 | 1 | 1 | 1 | 1 | 1 | 1 | 1 | 2 | 2 | 2 | 2 | 2 | 2 | 2 |
| 1 | 2 | 3 | 4 | 5 | 6 | 7 | 8 | 9 | 0 | 1 | 2 | 3 | 4 | 5 | 6 | 7 | 8 | 9 | 0 | 1 | 2 | 3 | 4 | 5 | 6 |

There are 31,536,000 seconds in a year. Currently, the next second is at your disposal. What are you going to do with it? In a second, you could decide to change the course of your life, forever. One second could mean the difference between earning a gold medal and doing a mere great effort that hardly anyone may recall.

Think about it. World-class athletes train long and hard to improve their speed by fractions of time. Most persons would recognize the name Michael Phelps, famed swimmer and winner of eight gold medals during the 2008 Olympics in Beijing, China. In dramatic fashion, he won the 100-meter butterfly event by one-hundredth of a second. Surprisingly, only 1.28 seconds separated Phelps, the first place winner, from the swimmer who placed last in the event. Time is important. Make each second count. Do it now!

There are 525,600 minutes in a year. Every minute has a potential dream that awaits an action to make it come to pass. By design, we yearn to produce. It's in our innermost being to excel and do great and mighty things.

Great feats can be achieved, records broken. In 1954, many believed that it was humanly impossible to run a mile in under four minutes. Physiologists said it would be dangerous to one's health. Roger Bannister broke the barrier when he eclipsed the long-standing hurdle at Oxford University's Iffley Road Track. He was clocked at 3'59.4" as he crossed the finish line. Then, the floodgates opened. The record would stand for only 46 days and by 1957, 16 runners had recorded sub-4-minute miles. The floodgates are open for you, too. Wake up and live your dream. Make each minute meaningful. Do it now!

> **"There are 525,600 minutes in a year. Every minute has a potential dream that awaits an action to make it come to pass."**

The past year, you had 8760 hours. What did you do with all of those hours? Some people work at least eight hours a day at a job that they don't like, around people who don't like them, to collect a paycheck that makes them question: Why? Time is structured in such a way that prompts us to make decisions to use it in a wise manner. Make a decision to use your time wisely. Every hour is important. Do it now!

Potentially, three-hundred and sixty-five days await you in the coming year. Each day is an opportunity – an opportunity to love; to do what's in your heart; to make a difference in the life of another. Design your day. Make your dreams come true. Stop waiting to excel. Go ahead and do it.

The first step is to begin. Write down one step. Attach two or three actions to it. Assign a time frame. Purpose in your heart to do it. If you fail to do it, try again. You must begin. You have to. Think of it like this: Although, the world keeps turning, the world is waiting on you to turn with it. No good deed that was ever done was done solely by or for one individual. Your actions will bless you and others. This is the power of giving your all.

You can do it. Do your dream— this second, this minute, this hour, today. This is the power. Do it now!

# ABOUT THE AUTHOR

Joey N. Jones is an accomplished educator who has inspired thousands to meet and exceed their goals by giving their all. He has captured this winning spirit in a clever, altogether useful and targeted way by identifying 100% positive words and phrases and linking them with successful others who have used the principles of success.

Dr. Jones earned B.S. and M.S. degrees in industrial arts/technology education from North Carolina A&T State University in Greensboro, North Carolina. After several years of successful teaching, he was fortunate to be awarded an academic fellowship to attend the University of Maryland in College Park, Maryland. There, he earned a Ph.D. degree in technology education/public school administration and supervision. He has since won numerous awards as a teacher and administrator.

Dr. Jones has a passion for the development of people, especially youth. He wears and has worn many hats—as a husband, father, teacher, principal, mentor, coach, motivational/inspirational speaker, carpenter, minister, and author. A native of Reidsville, North Carolina, he currently resides in Silver Spring, Maryland with his beautiful wife and three lovely, little girls. One of his favorite personal quotes is, "I refuse to be ignorant when knowledge is for the asking."

# REQUEST FOR MOTIVATIONAL AND INSPIRATIONAL SPEAKING ENGAGEMENTS

**Send requests to:**

Promo Publishers
P. O. Box 10091
Silver Spring, MD 20904

**Call:**

Toll Free: (877) 793-3538

**Email:**

info@promopublishers.com

# ADDITIONAL COPIES OF THIS BOOK MAY BE PURCHASED ON OUR DYNAMIC WEBSITE

www.promopublishers.com

## Selected References

Big George. (2008). *Big George bio*. Retrieved October 20, 2010 from http://www.biggeorge.com/main/bio.php

Black History Pages. (2008). *Dr. Patricia Bath*. Retrieved September 1, 2010 from http://www.blackhistorypages.net/pages/pbath.php

Bolden, T. (2008). *George Washington Carver*. New York: Harry N. Abrams, Inc.

Brilliant Dreams. (2008). *Twelve famous dreams*. Retrieved January 18, 2011 from http://www.brilliantdreams.com/product/famous-dreams.html

Buggs, S. (2007). *Business of giving*. Retrieved February 20, 2009 from http://www.chron.com/disp/story.mpl/business/buggs/4714442.html

Bureau of Labor Statistics. (2009). *Education pays*. Retrieved February 9, 2010 from http://www.bls.gov/emp/ep_chart_001.html

Capps, C. (1995). *The tongue, a creative force*. Tulsa, OK: Harrison House.

Carnegie Corporation of New York. (2010). *Our founder.* Retrieved October 20, 2010 from http://www.carnegie.org/about-us/foundation-history/about-andrew-carnegie/

Carson, B., & Murphey, C. (1992). *Think big: Unleashing your potential for excellence.* Grand Rapids, MI: Zondervan.

CoveyLink. (2009). *Leadership shortage.* Retrieved February 20, 2009 from http://www.coveylink.com/events-and-resources/ibi/leadership shortage

Covey, S. R. (1990). *The 7 habits of highly effective people.* New York: Fireside.

Dudley J. L. (2010). *Joe L. Dudley Sr., entrepreneur and humanitarian.* Retrieved September 6, 2010 from http://www.dudleyq.com/joedudley.html

Duplantis, J. (2008). *The everyday visionary, focus your thoughts, change your life.* New York: Touchstone/Howard Books.

Formula 409. (2010). *About us.* Retrieved November 4, 2010 from http://www.formula409.com/

Hammond, M. (2010). *Winner's way broadcast.* Retrieved December 17, 2010 from http://www.mac_hammond.org/Media/wwBroadcast.cfm

Haskins, J. (1995). *Black eagles: African Americans in aviation.* New York: Scholastic.

Hevesi, D. (2010). *Glen W. Bell, Jr., founder of Taco Bell dies at 86.* Retrieved January 22, 2010 from http://www.nytimes.com/2010/01/19/business/19bell.html

Hill, N. (2009). *Think and grow rich: 1937 Original version.* Norman Publishing.

Hotels.com. (2009). *The Ritz-Carlton.* Retrieved April 21, 2009 from http://www.hotels.com/hotel_the-ritz-carlton-washington-dc_171503_reviews.html

Howard, J.V. (2010). *Jim Valvano.* Retrieved June 19, 2010 from http://www.jimmyv.org/remembering-jim/jim-valvano-1946-1993.html

Inventor of the Week Archive. (2005). *Dr. Patricia Bath.* Retrieved September 1, 2010 from http://www.mit.edu/invent/iow/bath.html

Lowitt, B. (1999). *Bannister stuns world with 4-minute mile.* Retrieved January 17, 2010 from http://www.sptimes.com/news/121799/news_pf/sports/bannister_stuns_world.shtml

Mathews, J. (2010, April 4). He stood, delivered and changed our schools. *The Washington Post*, p. B2.

Microsoft. (2009). *Bill Gates: Chairman.* Retrieved January 30, 2010 from http://www.microsoft.com/presspass/exec/billg/?tab=biography

Murdock, M. (2006). *The uncommon leader: 31 keys for unlocking your greatness.* Fort Worth, TX: The Wisdom Center.

National Fatherhood Initiative. (2008). *The father factor: Facts of fatherhood.* Retrieved March 28, 2009 from http://www.fatherhood.org/father_father.asp

Nikebiz. (2011). *History and heritage.* Retrieved January 18, 2011 from http://www.nikebiz.com/company overview/history/1950s.html

Nobelprize. (2010). *Full text of Alfred Nobel's will.* Retrieved August 7, 2010 from http://www.nobelprize.org/alfred_nobel/will/will-full.html

Prince, D. (2004). Going the extra mile. *Harvest Times Online,* 4, 1-2. Retrieved February 17, 2010 from http://www.chc.org.sg/harvesttimes/ht_21/ht_21_01.asp

Rolex. (2011). *The world of Rolex.* Retrieved January 18, 2011 from http://www.rolex.com/en

Spruell, S., & Dudley, J. (2003). *Joe Dudley Sr. Dudley products.* Retrieved December 17, 2010 from http://money.cnn.magazines/fsb/fsb_archive/2003/12/01/359890/

The Idea Finder. (2005). *Paper clip history: Invention of the paper clip.* Retrieved March 29, 2009 from http://www.ideafinder.com/history/inventions/paperclip.htm

The 3M Company. (2009). *Who we are.* Retrieved April 13, 2009 from http://solutions.3m.com/wps/portal/3M/en_US/our/company/information/about-us/

USA Today.com. (2008). *Swimming results, 2008 Beijing Summer Olympics.* Retrieved January 17, 2010 from http://content.usatoday.com/sports/olympics/beijing/results/aspx?rsc=swm021100&ru=n

WD-40 Company. (2010). *Fascinating facts you never learned in school.* Retrieved November 4, 2010 from http://www.wd40.com/about-us/history/

Wikipedia. (2009). *Dream.* Retrieved May 16, 2009 from http://en.wikipedia.org/wiki/Dream

Wikipedia. (2010). *Jaime Escalante.* Retrieved July 30, 2010 from http://en.wikipedia.org/wiki/Jaime_Escalante

Wikipedia. (2011). *Rolex.* Retrieved January 18, 2011 from http://en.wikipedia.org/wiki/Rolex